"Offering both candor ... , ... Funding the Future defines well the current educational landscape and the significant challenges facing institutions and those who lead them. These current realities will require bold, collaborative, and courageous leaders who are willing to step into a new future filled with both peril and possibility. The breadth and scope of expertise represented in this book is impressive and the subject matter a 'must read' for educational leaders."

—**Brad Lau**, Vice President for Student Life, George Fox University

"I deeply value higher Christian education and I also bear the fiduciary responsibility of being a board member of a leading Christian university. From both perspectives I found *Funding the Future* challenging, motivating, and insightful. . . . The authors have done a masterful job of helping us think through the land mines that we can address before the crisis hits."

—**Roger Cross**, President Emeritus, Youth for Christ/USA

"*Funding the Future: Preparing University Leaders to Navigate the Coming Change* has been assembled by seasoned and wise voices from across the higher education landscape for 'such a time as this.' Relevant leaders must understand institutional finances, accounting rules, and decision-making models now more than ever. There is very little room for fiscal error, particularly for the majority of universities that rely heavily on tuition dollars to sustain their budgets."

—**Jay Barnes**, president, Bethel University, St. Paul, Minnesota

FUNDING THE FUTURE

The publication of this book has been sponsored by the
Association for Christians in Student Development.

ACSD   Association for Christians
in Student Development

FUNDING THE FUTURE

Preparing University Leaders to Navigate Impending Change

Stephen T. Beers

Timothy W. Herrmann

Paul Blezien

Editors

Abilene Christian University Press

FUNDING THE FUTURE
Preparing University Leaders to Navigate Impending Change

Contents

Foreword

The fall of 2008 brought a sea change in the country and in higher education. Assumptions held for years seemed no longer to be valid. The combination of significant demographic shifts and a changing economy notified leaders that a "new normal" was emerging. Early in 2008 would have been a good time to retire, but by the fall retirement accounts were shaken. Delayed retirements, increased pressure on financial aid, and rising fuel costs were among the many internal factors shaping this new normal. Collaboration and trust—obvious goals in campus decision making—were strained by the necessity to make hard choices about programs and personnel.

Funding the Future: Preparing University Leaders to Navigate the Coming Change has been assembled by seasoned and wise voices from across the higher education landscape for "such a time as this." Relevant leaders must understand institutional finances, accounting rules, and decision-making models now more than ever. There is very little room for fiscal error, particularly for the majority of universities that rely heavily on tuition dollars to sustain their budgets.

Leaders often cite the need to make mission-centered decisions. But when financial pressures arise, the meaning of "mission-centered" lies in the eye of the beholder. Times like these challenge institutions to define more clearly what is at the core of the mission as opposed to what may be a secondary good. Defining what is core must involve a collaborative campus discussion that will include trustees, as keepers of the mission, along with the faculty, staff, and administrators who will carry it out.

Chapter after chapter, this text is filled with thoughtful and practical advice for leaders in higher education. Finding better ways to discern collaboratively, sharpen the mission, gracefully care for people, and deepen our understanding of influential cultural trends is paramount to our future success and stability. The wisdom provided by these authors will help leaders in higher education do just that.

So, pray hard, breathe deeply, and grab all the wisdom you can from these good people! You'll be glad you did!

Jay Barnes, President
Bethel University
St. Paul, Minnesota

Acknowledgements

As is so often the case, credit for this publication is due to many more individuals than those showing up on the list of authors and we want to acknowledge some of these contributions and express our gratitude.

First, we thank the Association for Christians in Student Development for their generous support of this project. Without their initial encouragement and accompanying grant it would have been impossible even to initiate the work. We are also grateful for the guidance and encouragement of the executive committee. Their willingness to invest in this manuscript was not only critical to the authors but also demonstrates an organizational vision for providing resources that will help their members to more effectively lead and manage on their campuses.

Of course the greatest credit for the completion of this project is due those who agreed to author the various chapters. Each was selected because of the unique experience and valuable perspective that they bring to this work. We are humbled that the members of this very select group were willing to offer their time, knowledge, and wisdom to this effort.

The original research conducted for this project was a significant undertaking and, of course, involved a number of persons. Although we cannot disclose their identities, we are very grateful to the senior administrators who were willing to participate in the interview process that provided the data for this study. We are grateful that they were willing to invest the time and effort required. It is fair to say that they did so out of a desire to share their own experience and to help others to do their work more excellently. We also want to acknowledge Eileen Hulme of Azusa Pacific University for her technical assistance in the qualitative research design. This help was extremely valuable and without it we are certain that the resulting product would not have been as worthwhile.

A number of people helped with research, but Jessica Fankhauser from Taylor University and Philip Byers from Bethel University played especially significant roles in providing background support and research assistance. Jane Beers from John Brown University and Polly Graham from Indiana Wesleyan played a critical role by providing substantial editorial support and advice.

Of course, we would be remiss without expressing our gratitude to Leonard Allen and Abilene Christian Press for their feedback, advice, support, and, not least of all, patience. Similarly, we are grateful to our home institutions, John Brown University, William Jessup University, and Taylor University for their encouragement and support of this project and for being places where individuals work so tirelessly to steward the human and financial resources with which they have been entrusted.

Finally, we thank God for this opportunity, but even more for the opportunity to work in such a wonderful, meaningful, and incredibly rewarding vocation.

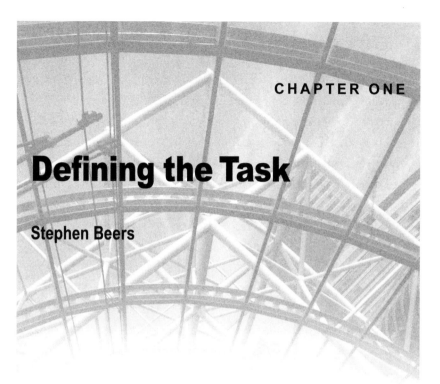

CHAPTER ONE

Defining the Task

Stephen Beers

Just a few years into the twenty-first century, higher educational leaders face unanticipated and unparalleled financial challenges. To start, federal and state support dwindles while universities suffer from volatile or negative growth projections on anemic endowments. In addition, the costs of "doing business" in private higher education continue to rise sharply. One only has to observe lagging faculty salaries and the unbridled healthcare costs to imagine the challenges of the private college administrator who is attempting to cultivate a distinctive, high quality institution. Furthermore, an economy stifled by private sector uncertainty and high unemployment has diminished the resources of donors and is crippling the average "consumer's" ability to pay even the most deeply discounted tuition. But ahead of the immediate response to a single economic downturn, what is most concerning to educational leaders is the question of the sustainability of the current financial model.

In addition to the specific financial challenges, the higher educational landscape is changing. The expanding local community college beckons from the next street corner, many high schools provide concurrent college credit, and every computer is now a portal for on-line education, whether for-profit or not-for-profit. Each of these new educational formats has the potential to impact the private university's enrollment efforts. State institutions, seeing the success of the private faculty-student ratio model, are adopting honors colleges and working to lower student number caps in some courses. Even the progress and expansion of the second- and third-world higher learning centers across the globe have the potential to impact head counts at some of our institutions.

At home on our campuses, things are changing as well. Student and family expectations have ballooned over the past decade to potentially unsustainable standards of quality. On the staffing side, many institutions have embraced the powerful, developmental methods of one-to-one mentoring, counseling, advising, and collaborative student and faculty research. But in the end, these important program additions create added expenses. Increases have not been limited to staffing. One has only to walk into a new residence facility to see unique amenities or peek into a renovated classroom to see the new technological additions as material examples of how expectations have increased. Although these additions have permitted educators both in and out of the classroom to perform their tasks more effectively, the ultimate evaluation cannot simply be about increasing effectiveness; it must also include questions about affordability and efficiency while fitting into a realistic economic plan for sustainability.

Another notable factor affecting the future of higher education involves the inclusion of a pedagogy that is more diverse and active. These changes in how we teach and where we teach are not about simply increasing comfort or changing the aesthetic of our campuses. Educational theorists as well as national and international educational leaders are challenging institutions of higher learning to move from a teacher-centered educational model, where institutions make sure that the instructor can be heard in a lecture hall, to a student-centered paradigm in which the formats and styles of both active and alternative learning will need to be accommodated. No one has the ability to predict just how this shift in pedagogy may impact our campuses and our enrollments.

Overview

This book, written by educational leaders currently in the fray, will encourage, inform, and guide a conversation critical for all private institutions across the country. It will enable leaders in the boardroom or at the directors' meeting to better understand the issues, more fully appreciate one another, and ultimately, embrace and engage in a collaborative process to manage change. This collaborative process capitalizes on the collective wisdom, knowledge, and commitment present in our institutions.

This book is organized into three sections: Gaining Perspective; Understanding Higher Education Finances; and Preparing for Change. Each section includes chapters that can be read in the context of the whole or as an individual thesis. Section one begins with a report on the original research done for this book titled "The Voice of Experience: A Phenomenological Study of Institutional Budgeting and Prioritization at Faith-based Higher Education Institutions," chapter two begins with a literature review of leadership decision-making processes in the light of complex financial pressures. The remaining portion of the chapter highlights the findings from a qualitative research project completed for this book. The research included a survey of senior executives of private higher educational institutions from across the United States. It explored the perspectives, priorities, and concerns that compose the higher educational leadership community's understanding of the challenges of funding private higher education. What surfaced was a more thorough understanding of how institutional leaders perceive the current financial challenge and how they believe we should prepare for change.

Sandwiched between the research findings and leadership recommendations, the second section, Understanding Higher Educational Finances, provides a practical yet critical primer on higher education's budgeting nomenclature and processes. We believe that too often educational leaders have been sidelined by a lack of basic knowledge of the budgeting process. After finishing these two chapters, readers may not be ready to assume the role of chief financial officer, but they will be better prepared to engage in critical financial discussions. Some readers may wish to pass over this section and read it last, since it is focused on establishing a baseline understanding of budgets and not on the leadership theory or practice outlined in the rest of the book.

In the third and final section, Preparing for Change, the five authors focus on vital leadership principles for navigating change. This section begins with an essay discussing ways to create a collaborative culture of discernment on your campus. The next two chapters address the importance of retaining a commitment to your institution's mission and managing difficult decisions with grace. The section ends with two chapters, one covering managing change while retaining a commitment to the institution's people and the final one providing a list of the critical issues educational leaders must address as they look to the future.

Our Hope

The editors hope that this text will first provide clarity in grasping and understanding the key financial issues impacting our institutions. Furthermore, we hope that the input from the diverse writers will spur institutional leaders to engage their colleagues more fully in order to understand the unique challenges each campus department faces. The intent of this work is to encourage and facilitate effective internal communication about institution-wide challenges. This increased communication will enable the institutional leadership to have a better understanding about how decisions will eventually impact the college's culture and mission.

We hope that this collaboration process will aid in activating the institution's leadership and avoid reactive decision-making influenced by fear, confusion, and turmoil. Instead, we believe that when administrators have the best information and are in a collaborative environment, they will work hard to implement difficult and necessary changes humanely.

Though the promise of a "prescriptive solution" is attractive, the authors recognize that the diversity of institutions and the unique conditions of varied geographic settings makes such "one size fits all" solutions untenable. Instead, this book offers resources intended to guide as a compass rather than to direct as a map, helping institutions to rediscover and maximize all available institutional resources: human, financial, and missional.

SECTION ONE

GAINING PERSPECTIVE

CHAPTER TWO

The Voice of Experience

A Phenomenological Study of Institutional
Budgeting and Prioritization at Faith-Based
Higher Educational Institutions

Paul Blezien and Polly Graham

*This chapter provides the reader with research data gathered specifically
for this book. A thorough review of the recent literature is followed by a
presentation of qualitative research that includes credible voices to provide
a confirmation of and/or contrast with the essays in this book.*

It is widely accepted that higher education is, at best, in a state
of heightened financial scrutiny and, at worse, in a state of financial
crisis.[1] Institutions are faced with declining or recovering endowments, escalating healthcare costs, and rising requests for financial
aid, all the while feeling the burden of waning state and federal
funding in an economically depressed market. As universities look
for ways to meet their financial demands, they are met with pressure
to keep tuition prices low. College costs have increased significantly

faster than both median household incomes and health insurance premiums.[2] The tuition predicament is especially an issue for private four-year colleges, as mounting evidence demonstrates that students are choosing more affordable community colleges and local public universities over their more expensive counterparts.[3] Other sections in this book provide more information to make the case that we are in difficult times. This section is a qualitative research piece that gives voice to those most involved with budget deliberations at their institutions. We will present findings from interviews with seven seasoned cabinet-level administrators at different faith-based higher educational institutions. These findings will follow a thorough review of the recent literature on budgeting and prioritization to determine whether there is any triangulation of emerging themes between the literature and the findings of our research.

Literature Review

Influences

To state that the financial issues facing higher education are complex and broad in scope will raise no contention. In 2008, when the credit crisis was at the forefront of administrators' concerns, institutions began wrestling through issues of liquidity, diversification in borrowing, and rising interest rates. Before this time, the focus of institutions was typically on maximizing investment returns, but the credit crisis brought about more scrutiny of previously relied upon strategies, specifically in the area of accessibility to funds. The credit crisis served as a stark reminder to institutions that they are not immune from market forces and that ignoring these forces could prove detrimental.[4]

Another casualty of current market trends is early retirements—professors are simply working longer. Many professors who are choosing to stay on longer than the traditional retirement age attribute their extended stay to financial need.[5] Ehrenberg speaks to the administrative challenges in this trend as he notes that many faculty members don't understand that as retirement age goes up the number of faculty must go down or that the level of faculty salary increase must lessen. Not surprisingly, most senior faculty members are not amenable to the idea of reducing their salary increases. This leaves administrators with the difficult job of finding funds to pay these costly salaries in a period of cutbacks and downsizing.[6]

Along with investment and personnel concerns, a variety of financially demanding issues compete for increasingly scarce resources. Issues such as deferred maintenance, rising technology costs, and sustainability initiatives are just a few of the additional financial considerations that college administrators and chief financial officers must address as they allocate institutional budgets.[7]

Communication and Budgetary Decision-making

As institutional administrators work to adjust to and survive the unfavorable financial realities, they are often faced with difficult budgetary decisions. Universities take two general approaches to making budgetary decisions: a top-down approach, where the president, board members, and administrators make decisions and then disseminate their decisions to other campus constituents, or a more collaborative approach, where campus constituents are involved in the decision-making process.[8] This latter approach is clearly favored by many at private liberal arts colleges.[9] However, each of these methods has strengths and limitations and function better in certain campus cultures.

In a top-down approach, the budget decisions are largely in the hands of the governing board, the president, and the administrators. Brinkman and Morgan affirm that this approach allows for expediency in decision-making, which is often necessary during crisis conditions.[10] Additionally, the top-down approach enables decisions to be made by those who have access to the data and understand the meaning of the data. However, this type of central-ized decision-making only functions well when there is a culture of trust. If faculty members distrust their administrators, it can lead to low morale and suspicion.[11] Suspicion is easily aroused when information is withheld from constituents. While it is often good practice to allay fears by sharing budgetary outlooks and decisions, Kent Chabotar recommends cautious communication, especially if decisions are tentative. Oftentimes, information shared with a faculty member or a small group of faculty members will then be passed on to others. As the information is communicated multiple times, it tends to get distorted or adapted, which leads to multiple interpretations of what the administrator actually said. When con-sidering the reality of imperfect communication paths, and the fur-ther problems that may arise from these phenomena, administrators may choose not to share information until absolutely necessary, even though it is not their desire to be clandestine.[12]

An alternative to the top-down budgeting approach is a col-laborative approach, which purposely involves various campus rep-resentatives in the budget-making process. The openness in this approach allows for increased understanding and acceptance of the budgetary decisions on the part of the campus community. It also promotes a sense of fairness. As campus employees are able to review and consider the logic behind the budgetary process at an early stage, it follows that the final budget may be more favorably received. Since faculty members are mediating a sizable portion of the budget, they should have intimate knowledge of what expendi-tures are absolutely necessary and what are expendable. According to Chabotar, budget committees should be broadly representative, including faculty, administrators, staff, support staff, and students. Also, members should be elected rather than appointed. Chabotar also asserts that transparency and multiple opportunities for input are important to a collaborative process. Thus, a committee should consider holding open meetings and providing other venues to solicit feedback.[13]

Collaborative budget making should be considered beyond its propensity to increase campus buy-in. According to the American Association of University Professors's (AAUP) statement "The Role of the Faculty in Budgetary and Salary Matters," faculty should be involved directly with budgetary decisions regarding curriculum, faculty status, and departmental equipment. However, in order to be fully vested in financial matters, faculty should be privy to pertinent information and be offered the opportunity to converse with administrators and the governing board. The AAUP's "Recommended Institutional Regulations on Academic Freedom" explicates how universities should proceed when they are faced with financial exigency. While it is clear that administrators and the governing board should play a key role in making decisions (especially those involving the termination of faculty appointments), the statement also makes clear that faculty should have primary responsibility in matters concerning both the criteria used for identifying who will be terminated and where within a specific program the dismissal should occur.[14] The AAUP's guidelines do not legally bind an institution unless its governing board has officially adopted them; however, the guidelines may serve as higher education "common law" if the institution is silent.[15]

Although there is clear benefit and merit in adopting a collaborative approach, there are pitfalls as well. Collaboration is rarely fast-moving—scheduling meetings, sharing information, and seeking input takes time. Additionally, involving many different voices in the process can result in stalemates and parties vying for their own interests rather than what is in the best interest of the university as a whole.[16] Ronald Ehrenberg asserts that oftentimes bias and self-interest will cloud the truth, resulting in a "tension between the expressed values of the university and the internal political maneuvering that takes place."[17] Furthermore, collaborative budgeting decentralizes the decision-making process, which diminishes administrative control. Especially in times of financial crisis when expediency is needed, administrators may have a harder time making immediate top-down decisions if their institution's modus operandi is collaborative.[18]

Mission-minded

Clearly linking budget allocation to institutional mission and goals is a best practice, especially in the current era of increased accountability.[19] However, Libby Morris argues that accountability is not the only reason there should be a focus on mission during budgeting allocations. If an institution uses its mission as a signpost in appropriating expenditures and making cutbacks, priorities will emerge that are defensible to critics. Being mission-minded also helps decision-makers decide how cuts should be administered. For example, would it be better to make strategic reductions or across the board cuts? Additionally, when it comes to making urgent decisions, an institution's mission can help classify priorities and, ultimately, help determine what must be preserved above all else.[20]

In order to ensure mission-aligned expenditures, Paul Brinkman and Anthony Morgan advise institutions to consider a combination of an "auto-pilot" approach with a zero-based approach. While a complete zero-based approach would be too time consuming, incorporating some zero-based budgeting allows institutions to take a fresh look at where institutional monies are going, and allows the opportunity for monies to be allocated substantially differently if need be.[21]

Making mission-centered decisions is not always black and white. William Massey highlights the imminent tension by pointing out that "universities exist to produce value rather than profit, but they also must wheel and deal in the marketplace."[22] Universities defy the market by financially supporting programs or personnel that are of missional value rather than market value. However, Massey warns that prioritizing missional endeavors requires discretionary spending. "Institutions without spending discretion cannot assert their values . . . . [Thus] nonprofits in serious financial difficulty tend to behave like for-profits."[23] One example of a market/mission tension is declining student interest in specific majors or departments. Especially at liberal arts institutions, decision-makers must weigh the cost of keeping shrinking departments, especially when those departments represent liberal arts values and thus align with their missions (e.g., foreign language) while growing departments are requesting funds for more faculty as student demand and class sizes increase.[24]

Policies

Barbara Lee contends that it is important to have varying policies and procedures in place so that the university is prepared when financially driven decisions need to be made. These procedures should address position shifts, job losses, reorganizing or terminating program offerings, and the roles that administrators and faculty play in these decisions. Planning can help address questions of who should be involved and what procedures should be followed. Lee suggests utilizing the AAUP's issued statements and guidelines when creating policies.[25]

Not having financial procedures in place prior to dire situations can result in what appear to be rash decisions. Woodward, Burchell, Wagner, and Knight warn that seemingly impulsive and highly reactionary decisions often lead to rifts between administrators and faculty. The rifts cultivate distrust, which worsens an already difficult situation. Therefore, it is important not to catch faculty members and other constituents by surprise. Being caught off guard, especially when policies are absent or not being adhered to, can result in not only faculty/administration conflict but could also lead to litigation. However, if procedures and policies are in place and utilized during healthy financial times, it will help alleviate imprudent decision making during difficult times.[26]

Summary

With a rising number of university consolidations, closings, and budget cuts, the reality is clear that institutions are facing financially hard times.[27] It is also likely that the financial pressures are here to stay, meaning that they will not just blow over once the market recovers. David Breneman believes that the current recession poses "serious questions about the values of our society and the strength of our commitment to educational opportunity."[28]

As institutions seek honorable and informed ways to respond, they must consider a variety of issues, all the while keeping up with their day-to-day responsibilities. As administrators and other university employees work to find suitable solutions, they are met with multiple pressures. They face the difficulty of remaining mission-focused while simultaneously responding to the market. They face the complex pressures involved in including and valuing multiple perspectives at the budgeting table while dealing with the reality that not everyone will agree. They face the conundrum of trying to keep financially afloat—which often involves raising tuition costs—without out-pricing the very students they need in order to keep their doors open. Breneman sends an especially ominous warning to liberal arts colleges, as he posits that it is probable that students will increasingly place less importance on the "fit" of a college and more on the price tag of tuition.[29] It seems that the call for creative fiscal problem solving could not be louder or clearer. In a time such as this, institutions should seek to ascertain and implement best practices while forming an innovative and feasible financial future.

So, it becomes important to solicit the wisdom of seasoned cabinet-level administrators specifically within our realm of private faith-based higher educational institutions to see if their perspectives align with what the literature has revealed. What follows is a report on the research conducted specifically for this book.

Research Method

A qualitative research method was employed for the purposes of this study. It is a phenomenological design intended to study the phenomenon of budgeting and institutional prioritization at faith-based colleges and universities in the United States. Specifically, the purpose was to examine those processes in the context of our current economic challenges.

Seven different seasoned cabinet-level leaders at faith-based higher educational institutions were selected to be interviewed for their perspectives on the institutional budgeting and prioritization process. Demographic information regarding the interview subjects will be presented in aggregate to ensure confidentiality. Five of the seven subjects were male and two were female. There was an even representation among the traditional cabinet-level positions. That is, president, provost/executive vice president, chief academic officer, chief advancement officer, chief enrollment officer, chief financial officer, and chief student development officer. Each of the subjects had served in more than one role or position in the course of their career. Collectively, those interviewed totaled 221 years of experience in faith-based higher education with approximately two thirds (141 years) of that time as cabinet-level administrators. They have served at fifteen different institutions all over the United States.

The interviews were conducted over the telephone and recorded with permission of the subjects. Each interview consisted of the same twelve questions and lasted approximately an hour and a half.

The recordings were transcribed, coded, and analyzed by two different researchers. The emerging themes reported in this research were a convergence of the two separate analyses of the data to ensure inter-rater reliability.

Research Results

Three primary themes emerged from the analysis of the interviews. The first of those themes involved an overarching blend of three sub-themes that will be referred to as the three Ts: trust, transparency, and truth. The second theme that emerged was the importance of connecting budget items, proposals, and requests to the strategic plan and mission of the institution. The third theme involved the concept of accountability and outcomes. The first two themes also appear in the literature review offering a triangulation of the data to enhance the validity of the findings.

Following the discussion of the emerging themes, the researchers will present perspectives on influencing factors that did not necessarily emerge as themes but were responses to specific questions in the interviews.

The Three Ts

It was difficult to separate trust, transparency, and truth from one another. The three concepts appear to be interrelated and integrated like three strands of a braided rope. The relationship between them was not sequential or linear. A "chicken or the egg" ambiguity exists. Interviewees were unclear whether it was trust that promotes transparency or transparency that breeds trust.

As the interview subjects shared their thoughts and feelings, it was clear that they had arrived at their high level of conviction as much from failures as from best practices. For example, they acknowledged the risks associated with being transparent in the process, but were more than willing to assume those risks rather than accept the certainty of the negative outcomes of exclusion and withholding information.

The importance of trust, transparency, and truth was discussed in light of both process and relationships. First and foremost was the relationship among the primary decision-makers. "I would say that one of the things that helps with difficult decision-making is to have a cabinet that has developed a high level of trust with each other. The most important thing in prioritization may be the relationships you bring to it." It is interesting to note that this quote was from the interview subject whose primary role was chief financial officer.

Trust was also expressed as an important factor in relationships beyond the cabinet. When given the opportunity to express one wish that would improve institutional budgeting and prioritization, one interviewee shared this: "It would be that the magic wand would be waived over the community and they would all have a trust of their leaders to see the big picture clearly. Because . . . no matter how transparent we try to be, no matter how we try to over communicate, if it started with a lack of trust it doesn't matter." Similarly, another expressed this wish: "I would wave the magic wand over everybody so they would have trust in the leadership, that even though they may not understand the direction [or rationale], they still have the faith and trust to know that [leadership] will fulfill the ultimate goal—even if they don't understand why a particular decision was made." Interview subjects expressed varying notions of this idea but all with a similar deeply felt desire to be trusted. There was a clear understanding of the relationship between transparency and trust but, as stated above, not a great deal of clarity as to which was the cause and which was the effect.

The commonly held conception of budget deliberations as an adversarial exercise was viewed as clearly dysfunctional by those interviewed. They spoke of an alternative perspective involving collaborative discernment. This concept has been expanded upon in chapter five. Rather than each cabinet member, division, or department being in battle against one another for institutional resources, it was deemed healthier and more productive to view all participants as joined in battle against the problems—budget and otherwise—facing the institution.

As the issue of transparency was discussed there was a very clear understanding of the importance of truthful expression and administration of this openness. This emphasis on truth was much more about clarity and openness than it was about duplicity or outright lying. Boundaries to transparency were acknowledged, but nothing definitive was offered as to where those boundaries are. It would appear that the discernment necessary to determine how transparent an institution might be depended on factors specific to each institution.

Another factor in the discussion of transparency was the level of involvement of non-cabinet-level faculty and staff in the budget development process. No consistent message developed about what that should specifically look like. However, there was a clear sense that presidents and their cabinets need to be intentional about this as they develop their institutional budget development and prioritization process. That intentionality must include a well-developed rationale that is clearly understood by all stakeholders.

Mission and Strategic Plan

"We ought to ask ourselves whether in fact the budget as it came out or as it's being formed or even how we did the budget truly reflects our mission and values. If it doesn't, then that should be a wake-up call to us. I think we also have to be much more deliberate about linking our budget to our strategic priorities."

This observation from one of the interview subjects illustrates much of what was said about the linkage between the budget and the mission/strategic plan. They stressed not merely using the mission as a guide to the end product of an institutional budget but also factoring the mission into the budget development process. If the budget development and prioritization process is a difficult journey through treacherous and potentially uncharted territory, then our strategic plan and mission serve as a map and compass. The strategic plan is a map that helps guide us to the fulfillment of institutional goals while the mission serves as a compass constantly reminding us of "true north" or what is most important.

In the same way that one can learn much about a person's values by looking at his/her checkbook and credit card statements, one can also tell much about an institution by looking at its budget. This sound bite from one of the interviews says it concisely: "The budget essentially is a financial statement about a school's institutional priorities and mission."

By focusing on the strategic plan, one can also exercise another perspective that was deemed as essential to an effective budget development and prioritization process. The interview subjects spoke frequently about being future oriented when involved in budget deliberations. Sustainability was a term that was used consistently throughout the interviews. The ability to manage more than one year's budget at a time appears to be integral to sound budgeting. They shared a number of examples of how difficult financial challenges were attacked over a period of multiple budget years. The strategic plan provided a structure to make the complexities of being future oriented manageable. One helpful image was offered—the idea of looking at a video as opposed to a snapshot. Seeing where the budget has been and is headed was more helpful than looking at a particular year in isolation.

Another positive aspect of integrating mission and the strategic plan into the budget deliberations was to have a strong frame of reference to navigate the difficult balance between parts of the budget that are missional and those that are revenue generating. It was not that these two dimensions are mutually exclusive but that each appears to be on a continuum and not necessarily dichotomous. For example, a department, position, or other expenditure cannot be classified simply as missional or not missional. There would seem to be degrees of connection to the mission. Determining the degree of connection to the mission is obviously more difficult than measuring the capacity of revenue generation. Once those have been established, it is even more challenging to engage the next step—blending the two criteria. One interviewee shared a specific example of a conversation considering whether tenure decisions should make allowances for those faculty members who are recruiters in a given major. Another summarized it in the following manner: ". . . you look at what are those things that are *really* missional that may be a drain on resources but we just have to do it. Then what are those things that are missional that provide resources. And we just debate and discuss whether those things that are the highest priority for us actually, and to what degree, fulfill our [mission]."

Accountability and Outcomes

"I think we need to be able to more than ever translate our budgets and the way we will spend our money into outcomes." There was a degree of overlap with this theme and the issues of collaboration mentioned in the theme of trust, transparency, and truth. Involving various constituencies and stakeholders in budget deliberations as presenters of proposed increases in existing budgets or even new programs/positions was seen as integral to holding budget mangers accountable for outcomes that they themselves had proposed.

So, involving faculty in the budget development process may be less about buy-in than it is about being able to discern whether a program or proposal should continue to be funded. Another factor in the involvement of budget managers is to have them provide first-hand perspective on the level of connection of a program to the mission of the school. Admittedly biased, it still is valuable in shedding some light on the often challenging task of assessing the missional nature of a budgeted/proposed item.

The clear message was that budgeted or proposed programs and personnel had to somehow create outcomes favorable to fulfilling the strategic plan and advancing the mission. The interview subjects understood that this is a laborious process that can be demoralizing when much time is invested into departmental budget preparations and then the funds are not approved. Even with this concern, there was a strong feeling that higher educational institutions needed to create an environment where people developed budgets and pro-posals with specific and measurable outcomes in mind. Further, all involved needed to understand that evaluation and accountability would be part of the process and factor into future funding deci-sions. A few of the interviewees bemoaned the fact that although they spent much time and energy determining proposed outcomes, they did not have a definitive mechanism or process in place to evaluate whether budgeted items had indeed achieved their stated outcome. This flaw negates the value of outcomes discussions and jeopardizes budget development and deliberation exercises.

Influencing Factors

Specific questions were asked during the interviews regarding the role of the president of the institution in the budget development process. In addition, interviewees were asked to reflect on what influence, if any, the faith tradition of the school had on the budget process. They were also asked to comment on how current economic

challenges affected, if at all, their recent institutional budget deliberations. They were also asked an open-ended question regarding
any other influencing factors that affected budget decisions.

In regard to the role of the president in institutional budgeting and prioritization, the interviews revealed a continuum of
presidential engagement and involvement. They expressed varying
preferences for where presidents ought to be on that continuum
from autocratic to laissez-faire, with most desiring something
in the middle. There was a clear expectation on the part of all
interview subjects that the president must own the process and
its decisions.

> Here are the principles that need to [be considered] no
> matter where they fall on that continuum. They need to
> *own* it. When all is said and done, they need to own what-
> ever decisions were made in regard to the budgets, budget
> cuts, budget builds, etc. That's very important and most
> presidents understand that . . . . one of the principles is
> they need to own it, they need to champion the process that
> went into it . . . and believe that it was the best it could have
> been. To me that's one of the big roles the president has to
> play: owning the decisions, championing the process, and
> believing that it's the best it could have been.

Ownership of the budget by the president, as it was described in
the interviews, was specifically characterized by the following: do
not merely leave budget and decision-making processes to the CFO,
provide clarity regarding linkage to the mission and strategic plan,
exercise a judicious use of authority, and determine the relevant
constituencies and ensure they are heard.

Identifying the ways in which the faith tradition of the school
influenced the budget decisions was a real struggle for the interview subjects. There was little in the way of connection to the

specific denominational affiliation of the respective institutions. The items that were mentioned were tied most directly to broader issues of the Christian faith. So, stewardship was mentioned frequently and in various contexts. There was a prevailing thought that the decisionmakers accounted to a higher authority than each other, representative constituencies, or even the board. In addition to the idea of stewardship, there was also a sense that our common faith supported the idea of collaborative discernment. "The idea of a body of believers acting together matters," was the way one of the interviewees described it.

The open-ended question regarding other influences on budget decisions and processes yielded many interesting responses, but the only one that was mentioned with any consistency was the board of trustees. In the most positive sense, they were able to provide significant guidance and input into the broad parameters of the institutional budget—tuition pricing, salary increases, and capacity issues (i.e. tripling dorm rooms), for example. They could be less than helpful when advocating for "pet projects." This included providing a substantial donation that would only partially pay for a building or program, leaving the remainder to be funded through the operational budget.

So, how about the current economic challenges? What level of impact have they had on institutional budgeting processes, decision making, and prioritization? How has thinking changed? What have we learned? Have we improved? The clear theme that emerged from this portion of the interviews was that "there is nothing new under the sun." The economic crisis has only put in sharp relief what many would already acknowledge as wise approaches to budgeting processes and decisions. It was hypothesized in more than one interview that the strength of the economy before the downturn afforded us the luxury of being less than totally faithful to a deliberate and thorough process that forced us into difficult decisions.

There was also a feeling that the economic crisis has contributed to a heightened sense of urgency in applying the concepts of sound budgeting. One interviewee summarized it well:

> How many times have we heard someone say "don't waste a good crisis."? It's not that you look forward to these things, but the reality is we were forced to make some decisions that we probably would have avoided if we could. There were some decisions that we knew needed to be made and have had a crying need to be addressed for more than a decade. When the fall of 2008 happened we realized that we could no longer avoid those even though they had some unpleasant consequences for certain programs . . . . Therefore, if there are hard decisions to make, it's better to make them sooner rather than later and to the degree that we delay making a decision that we really should make we are not helping the institution.

Recommendations

Thinking about next steps can be daunting when considering the findings of the literature review and the qualitative study conducted for this book. At least one clear message emerges from all the research presented here: *It's about time!* There are two ways to view this message. The first way is simply the commonly held meaning of this phrase: something to the effect of, "What took you so long?" The answer to that question is that we have been distracted from the problems and dysfunctions in our budgeting and prioritization decisions by our relative prosperity. That certainly sheds some light on our current status as recent economic challenges and crises have unfolded.

The second way to view the message, "It's about time," is to take a more literal interpretation. One might say that time is the critical issue integral to all of what has been learned in this research. We will find ourselves unable to utilize the wisdom presented unless we intentionally and strategically allot the time necessary to practice what we have learned. There is not one item on the list below that does not have a significant "time on task" component.

- Establish relationships of trust within the cabinet
- Establish relationships of trust within the campus community (i.e. faculty and administration)
- Build collaboration and broad-based input into the budget process
- Ensure clarity and transparency in communicating budget processes, decisions. and rationale
- Incorporate anticipated outcomes into discussions about budget proposals
- Develop mechanisms of accountability to determine whether anticipated outcomes were realized
- Provide the necessary space for discussions that determine linkages between budgeted/proposed items and the mission and strategic plan

The last item presumes that there is actually a clearly articulated and commonly understood mission and strategic plan. If this is not the case, then that may be the necessary place to start. The challenge of that can be overwhelming. Taking on a task like that in the middle of an economic crisis can be a bit like asking the mechanic to work on the engine of our bus while traveling down the interstate. But if we are serious about arriving at our destination, we have to know where we are headed. As great as it might feel just to be moving, we may not feel so great about the direction we are headed based on the instincts of a few in the front of the bus. Wouldn't it have been great if someone had just paused to ask for help? Or worse yet, we may be very disappointed to see where we end up if the bus actually breaks down and quits running altogether.

The level of effort and difficulty required to navigate the challenges of effective institutional decisionmaking regarding the budget is monumental, especially when tempted by shortcuts that many advise against. For example, across the board cuts take much less time to administer than the recommendations above, but we are hard pressed to find experienced leaders who see this as a wise course of action. One interview subject put it in perspective with the following image: "Across the board cuts could be described as a band-aid at best and a placebo at worst. Neither is effective at ultimately curing the ailment."

Ultimately much of what has been revealed in the research conducted for this section is general wisdom that is applicable whether in a state of crisis or not. It is a message of faithfulness to the process and the people involved. The wisdom is simple in its presentation but so difficult in its application. The learning and recommendations are easy to ignore when things are going well. It is also easy to become distracted from what we know to be best when in a period of crisis and the leanness that comes with it. The best way to do something is rarely the easy or fast way. Consider this a call to faithfulness regardless of the circumstances that you and the institution you serve are experiencing. Institutional budgeting is an opportunity to develop the people being led and served by your school as well as a catalyst for advancing its mission and purpose.

Endnotes

1. Paul T. Brinkman and Anthony W. Morgan, "Financial Planning: Strategies and Lessons Learned," *Planning for Higher Education* 38, no. 3 (April–June 2010): 6; Susan W. Engelkemeyer, "Resources for Managing Our Institutions in These Turbulent Times," *Change* 36, no. 1 (Jan.–Feb. 2004): 53; Libby V. Morris, "Budget Cuts 101: Performance and Priorities," *Innovative Higher Education* 33, no. 4 (January 01, 2009): 215.

2. Olin L. Adams III, and David M. Shannon, "Cost Control: The Imperative for Higher Education," *College and University* 81, n. 4 (Jan. 1, 2006): 61; David W. Breneman, "For Colleges, This is Not Just Another Recession." *Chronicle of Higher Education* 48, no. 40 (June 14, 2002). http://chronicle.com/article/For-Colleges-This-Is-Not-Just/27351/ (accessed May 25, 2011); Brinkman and Morgan, "Financial Planning," 13; Sara Hebel, "Bill Clinton Urges Colleges to Strive for Solutions at Home and Abroad," *Chronicle of Higher Education*. http://chronicle.com/article/Bill-Clinton-Urges-Colleges-to/65073/ (accessed June 1, 2011).

3. Peter McPherson and David Shulenburger, "University Tuition, Consumer Choice and College Affordability: Strategies for Addressing a Higher Education Affordability Challenge." *NASULGC Discussion Paper* (Nov. 2008): 29–30. http://www.aplu.org/NetCommunity/Document.Doc?id=1296 (accessed May 20, 2011); Karin Fischer, "Crisis of Confidence Threatens Colleges," *Chronicle of Higher Education* 57, no. 37 (May 20, 2011). http://chronicle.com/article/Higher-Education-in-America-a/127530/ (accessed June 1, 2011).

4. Adams III and Shannon, "Cost Control," 61; Goldie Blumenstyk and Kelly Field, "Credit Squeeze Exposes Weaknesses in College Investment Strategies," *Chronicle of Higher Education* 55, no. 8 (October 17, 2008). http://chronicle.com/article/Credit-Squeeze-Exposes/5908/ (accessed May 30, 2011).

5. Breneman, "What Colleges Can Learn From Recessions Past," *Chronicle of Higher Education* 55, no. 7 (October 10, 2008). http://chronicle.com/article/What-Colleges-Can-Learn-From/16846/ (accessed May 30, 2011).

6. Ronald G. Ehrenberg, "Adam Smith Goes to College: An Economist Becomes an Academic Administrator," *Journal of Economic Perspectives* 13, no. 1 (Winter 1999): 110.

7. Brinkman and Morgan, "Financial Planning," 6; Ehrenberg, "Adam Smith Goes to College," 111.

8. Kent J. Chabotar, "Managing Participative Budgeting in Higher Education," *Change* 27, no. 5 (Sept.–Oct. 1995). http://www.eric.ed.gov/ERICWebPortal/detail?accno=EJ514958 (accessed May 20, 2011).

9. Phillip W. Feerar, "The Impact of the Recent Financial Downturn on Private Liberal Arts Colleges" (Unpublished disseratation, Pennsylvania State University, 2005), 160.

10. Brinkman and Morgan, "Financial Planning," 11.

11. Chabotar, "Participative Budgeting."

12. Ibid.; Ehrenberg, "Adam Smith Goes to College," 111.

13. Cindy S. Volk, Sheila Slaughter, and Scott L. Thomas, "Models of Institutional Resource Allocation," *Journal of Higher Education* 72, no. 4 (July–August 2001): 408; Chabotar, "Participative Budgeting."

14. William J. Woodward, Eileen Burchell, Donald R. Wagner, and Jonathan Knight, "Financial Exigency, Academic Governance, and Related Matters," *Academe* 9, no. 2 (March–April 2004): 104–112.

15. Barbara A. Lee, "Colleges Should Plan Now for a Financial Crunch," *Chronicle of Higher Education* 50, no. 42 (June 25, 2004). http://chronicle.com/article/Colleges-Should-Plan-Now-for-a/26859/ (accessed May 30, 2011).

16. Chabotar, "Participative Budgeting"; William F. Massey and Robert Zemsky, "Faculty Discretionary Time: Departments and the 'Academic Ratchet,'" *Journal of Higher Education* 65, no. 1 (Jan.–Feb. 1994). http://www.jstor.org/pss/2943874 (accessed March 21, 2011).

17. Ehrenberg, "Adam Smith Goes to College," 106.

18. Chabotar, "Participative Budgeting."

19. Engelkemeyer, "Resources for Managing," 53; Feerar, "Recent Financial Downturn," 160.

20. Morris, "Budget Cuts 101," 216.

21. Brinkman and Morgan, "Financial Planning," 10.

22. William F. Massey, "Collegium Economicum: Why Institutions Do What They Do," *Change* 36, no. 4 (July–August 2004): 28.

23. Ibid., 33.

24. William R. Johnson and Sarah Turner, "Faculty without Students: Resource Allocation in Higher Education," *Journal of Economic Perspectives* 23, no. 2 (Spring 2009): 186–187.

25. Lee, "Colleges Should Plan Now."

26. Woodward, et al., "Financial Exigency."

27. Lee, "Colleges Should Plan Now."

28. Breneman, "For Colleges, This is Not Just Another Recession."

29. Breneman, "What Colleges Can Learn From Recessions Past."

UNDERSTANDING HIGHER EDUCATIONAL FINANCES

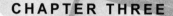

CHAPTER THREE

Four Important Concepts that Impact Higher Educational Finances

Patricia Gustavson

Gaining even the most rudimentary understanding of how the private university's budgets work is critical in being able to appropriately dialogue and influence change. This chapter provides some important financial concepts in preparing educational leaders to maximize their roles.

The following four concepts are basic to higher education finances. As simple as they may seem, they are often misunderstood or inadequately considered by college leaders. The concepts below are by no means exhaustive, but they provide language and understanding for institution-wide conversations. More importantly, they provide a focus for board members, administrators, and academic leaders who want to design a customized list of critical indicators for their own campuses.

Concept One: Non-profit

In a for-profit organization, each department understands the predominant goal: to create a reasonable profit for the owners or investors. It is understood that there is a "bottom line," and that each decision will be evaluated based on its impact on profits. However, when there is no commonly accepted bottom line, it is harder to measure the value of competing financial decisions. Mission statements and strategic goals can help to provide focus, but differences in interpretation and perceived priorities remain.

One president in my experience sought to encourage campus staff to strive to achieve the highest and best results in each department. As a motivational goal, he challenged us all to make the university "world class." This meant very different things to different people. The choir director seized this challenge to press for new music facilities and for more rehearsal hours. The soccer coach insisted that a world-class program was going to require lights on the soccer field. The admissions director requested vehicles for each admissions counselor. Each academic department, of course, had its own set of perceived needs. Every non-profit institution has a long list of goals, but prioritizing them makes decision-making more complicated and nuanced than in a "bottom line" environment.

Non-profit status in higher education means that a college is exempt from paying taxes on revenues related to its tax-exempt purpose. Most colleges reference Internal Revenue Code Section 501(c)(3) for justifying their tax-exempt status. This allows them to avoid paying income taxes on tuition and most other student charges and revenue sources; it also allows them to receive gifts from individuals and corporations who can then claim those gifts as tax exemptions.

This classification is allowed by the IRS because of the charitable purposes served by colleges, namely the post-secondary education of academically qualified students, many of whom might not be able to afford that education.

Incorporation as a not-for-profit does not guarantee tax-exemption for all revenues, nor does it come without some strings attached. "Unrelated Business Income" is the term for any revenue generated by a college's activities that do not directly relate to its tax-exempt purpose of educating students. An example might be selling memberships to non-students for the use of college exercise facilities. If the main purpose of this activity is to generate revenue, especially if there are similar for-profit facilities in the community, the college may have to pay taxes on the related revenues. This is one of many reasons that good ideas for new programs should be discussed with business and legal staff early in the planning process.

Because there is a great benefit in being exempt from paying income taxes and in being able to receive gifts, a growing number of regulations and standards are attached to the continuation of an institution's tax-exempt status. Donors, board members, and employees cannot derive inappropriate personal benefit from transactions with the college. Presidents cannot be paid above the range for presidents at comparable institutions without clear justification. Greater accountability and transparency is expected from organizations that have been granted not-for-profit status.

Concept Two:
Balanced Budget

Leaders with experience in for-profit organizations generally understand the importance of a balanced budget. Those working in the institution with limited exposure to the budget process can sometimes seem resistant to the balanced budget implication that "money is everything." The variety of goals and priorities in a not-for-profit organization can blur the fact that there is still a financial bottom line. For most private colleges, resources are limited. The budget process begins by establishing realistic revenue expectations. Expenses should then be set within this context. Revenue expectations should never be optimistically inflated to cover desired expenses.

That doesn't mean that a budget can never be proposed that results in a net deficit for the year. If there have been past years of net surpluses, an operating reserve may exist that provides for the luxury of spending more than can be covered with revenues for a given fiscal period. But practical reality and prudence require that revenues be projected realistically and that expenditures generally be covered by revenues. The following is a quick guide to the major revenue categories and the largest single expense category at most private institutions.

Gross Tuition Revenue

The primary source of revenue in most colleges is tuition. If a college charges a blanket amount of tuition per term, the gross tuition revenue for the year will be the number of Annual Average Full Time Equivalent (AAFTE) students multiplied by the tuition charge per year. For colleges that charge per credit hour, the gross tuition equals the expected number of credit hours multiplied by the tuition charge per credit hour. Some campuses may have differential charges for different programs or may have a blend of blanket tuition and credit hour/unit tuition. The key is that each campus must determine an accurate way to predict its gross tuition revenue from year to year. The process is complicated by part-time students, different enrollment levels in different terms, changes in attrition rates, shifts in graduation rates, and other such factors. It is important to have a time-tested model that is sufficiently rigorous for reliably projecting tuition units.

After tuition, there are other categories of revenue that will vary in importance from one campus to another. These would include gifts for operational purposes, revenues from auxiliary operations including student room and board charges, allowable spending amounts from endowment investments, and miscellaneous fees and other income sources. As with tuition, the contribution of each revenue category must be projected for the next fiscal year in the budget process. Conservative budgeting mandates that recent past historical data be used to make these projections. Unless there is a very clear upward trend that is likely to be sustained, or unless there is a strong argument justifying a greater contribution from any revenue source, increases should not be assumed. That means that the tuition charge can be increased and reflected in the projected budget, for instance, but it should not be assumed that the number of new students will increase or that giving will be greater.

Marginal Net Revenue

One of the best set of questions I was ever asked as a business officer by a president boils down to: "How much revenue do we receive per student, and how is that trending?" It took accounting staff several months, in consultation with other departments, to pull together the relevant data to answer that question accurately. The issues that had to be defined included:

- What revenues (tuition, fees, etc.) should be included as gross tuition for each fiscal year?
- Which scholarships should be subtracted from gross tuition in calculating net tuition?
- How should the number of Financial Full Time Equivalent students be calculated?

The end result was a series of graphs showing all categories of operational revenues and expenditures on a per student basis. It provided clear graphic images for ten years showing the impact of rising enrollment, rising unfunded discount rate, and relatively flat other sources of revenue such as endowment spending, gifts, auxiliary net revenues, and other revenues. Most of all the results of this process gave the campus a common language for talking about the financial impact of decisions at a fairly sophisticated level.

The concept of marginal net revenue helps those in non-profit organizations to think and talk in a practical way about financial realities. Important issues of mission alignment, academic quality, constituency expectations, institutional traditions, competitive factors, and other strategic values can be given their place in decision-making, but the marginal net revenue concept helps to keep everyone's eye on the critical value of ongoing financial viability.

Restricted Funds Revenue (and Expenses)

Tax law allows donors to make gifts to not-for-profit organizations and to restrict the purpose of those gifts. It is the recipient organization's responsibility to be sure that the donor's gift is used per the donor's direction. The person giving a restricted gift may be a complete outsider to the organization or may be a board member or employee, but he or she must be acting as an outsider when the restricted gift is made. No individual or group acting inside the organization can undo such a restriction. This is sometimes counterintuitive to board members, who are accustomed to organizations in which all funds are under the discretionary control of the leadership. The board, of course, can mandate that funds be set aside for specific purposes, but this does not create a true restriction. Such funds are termed "board-designated."

Restrictions can be a direct relief to the operational budget, or they can present challenges to that budget. In a worst case scenario, they should be declined. As an example, consider a donor who makes a gift restricted for student scholarships. The college may have initiated a special fundraising campaign for this purpose, or the gift may offset scholarships that would otherwise have been covered in the operational budget. Such a gift obviously provides clear budget help. If the donor further restricts the gift, perhaps for business majors from Kansas, it may require more careful handling but may still provide budget relief. If a number of students come from Kansas and major in business, the financial aid office will want to be sure to award the restricted funds first. If the donor wants to provide scholarships for students in a curricular or co-curricular program that does not yet exist, using the gift as leverage to encourage the initiation of such a program, it becomes "a gift that eats." This is a "gift" that would create additional budget expenditures.

Restricted gifts may create tension between departmental staff and the campus leadership that will have to be handled on a case-by-case basis. Well-intentioned donors often make gifts restricted to specific departments or programs of their preference. The involved faculty or staff members want to see those gifts used to provide budget above and beyond the existing level. Administrators and boards often want to use these gifts for budget relief, using the restricted funds to offset budgeted expense amounts. A balance must be struck between the reality of limited resources and the encouragement of the generosity of donors.

Institutional Scholarships and Discount Expenses (or Unrestricted Expenses)

There are many different kinds of student financial aid. This may be one of the reasons that misunderstandings abound among parents, students, and even college faculty and staff about the availability of scholarships and their sources. Some parents and prospective students are relieved to learn that there are ways to attend the college of their choice without paying the full "sticker price." Others have been advised by friends and acquaintances that a seemingly bottomless pit of scholarship money is at the fingertips of the financial aid counselors. All one has to do is negotiate aggressively for it.

There are external sources of financial help for students including federal Pell grants and Title IV funds in the form of grants, loans, and work-study. The Pell grants or other external, third-party scholarships that are awarded directly to specific students are not of direct budgetary concern; they simply represent external sources of payment for the student's charges. The federal funds for grants, work, or loans that are disbursed to the college are awarded to students selected by the campus financial aid office according to relevant criteria. These are restricted funds.

In addition, state grant programs, foundation or organizational grants, restricted gifts, and the spending from restricted endowment funds all may provide funding for student scholarships. They may be targeted for students with financial need or they may target particular student characteristics such as academic performance, major, home state, co-curricular involvement, or other such criteria.

Beyond such restricted sources of student financial aid, most institutions provide additional unrestricted or "unfunded" scholarships to students; this budgeted amount of the gross tuition is basically an institution's discount rate. These scholarships may be awarded to students with financial need or they may be merit-based, awarded to students who will bring desired characteristics to the student body. Merit scholarships may be awarded for the student's past academic performance in high school or on standardized tests, for students who agree to participate in co-curricular activities such as athletic teams or music groups, for service in leadership positions on campus, or any other criteria determined by the college. The total amount of unrestricted or unfunded student scholarships awarded to students divided by the total tuition revenue recognized in the same time period is the *unfunded discount rate*, expressed as a percentage. Gross tuition, as stated earlier, is the total tuition charged to all students for a specified fiscal period. Net tuition then is the gross tuition revenue less institutionally funded and controlled student grants.

Current accounting standards for higher education require that scholarships be shown as a contra-revenue, a discount from tuition revenue. Unfunded scholarships represent a deduction that must be made from gross projected tuition revenue before building an expense budget. Because many scholarships come from restricted sources, faculty and others may fail to understand the direct competition between unrestricted, unfunded student scholarships and departmental budgets. There is often pressure on the student financial aid office to make aid packages attractive enough to bring in more new students or to provide more help to students who are already enrolled. When the funding source for these scholarships is the general operational budget, everyone involved needs to understand the trade-offs.

Awarding aid in fluctuating enrollment climates is a real challenge. A budget is built based on a projected number of new and continuing students. An amount for unfunded student scholarships is part of the budget for most colleges. As new students apply and as continuing students make their intentions known, the student financial aid staff builds aid packages that may include loans, work assignments, restricted scholarships, and unrestricted scholarships. This rolling process is full of uncertainties, particularly with regard to the new students. On the one hand, if all available budgeted unrestricted scholarships are awarded and if the incoming class is smaller than expected, net tuition will fall below what is budgeted. On the other hand, if the financial aid staff award only the budget available, they may lose additional students who might have enrolled with modest scholarship levels. Each campus should have a team of admissions, student financial aid, and business office representatives who review trends and create aid award guidelines involving the desired unfunded discount rate while maximizing net tuition revenue and allowing for enrollment growth.

Concept Three: Unseen Budget Influences

In any budget there are expenses that are harder to see yet significantly influence revenues and expenses. Below are three that illustrate that concept and have a significant impact.

Subsidy

The nonprofit higher education industry is full of subsidies. For example, if a college charges a flat rate for one or more meal plans, the student who eats three meals daily in the cafeteria and goes back for seconds is subsidized by the student who has an occasional bowl of cereal for lunch and dinner. The student who participates in intramurals, makes use of counseling services, or requires a great deal of disciplinary intervention is subsidized by the student who is less involved with campus activities and takes less staff time. Students who have large amounts of unfunded student aid may be subsidized by those who pay in full. If the tuition charge is the same for all majors, the music major with small classes and private lessons or the engineering major with extensive equipment support may be subsidized by history or English majors in larger classes requiring less equipment. This subsidy, based on the different costs in majors, may be a significant issue at institutions desiring to add programs or adjust away from expensive majors.

Many campuses try to address some of these apparent inequities by developing differential charges or special fees. Students and their parents are increasingly informed and proactive as consumers. This is enhanced by the increasing presence of for-profit institutions in higher education. They offer a different product, stripped of much of the programming and services provided by traditional campuses. This results in cost comparisons and greater scrutiny of cost and value.

It is important that campus decision-makers periodically review subsidy issues. This involves knowing the numbers of students who benefit from each program or service, the value and importance of the outcomes of the program or service, and the costs involved. Often a finer level of revenue and cost detail will be necessary than is provided by routine financial reports. As non-traditional and for-profit competitors continue to provide lower cost college credits, degrees, and career entry opportunities, traditional higher educational institutions will need to understand and communicate effectively regarding their offerings and costs. The concept of subsidy is important as each campus makes decisions in the planning and budgeting process about which programs to initiate, retain, enhance, or discontinue.

Indirect Costs for New Programs

The majority of programs and departments in the academic area and many of the programs and departments in the student development area pursue the primary mission of the college, namely the academic, occupational, social, emotional, and spiritual development of the students through the curriculum and the co-curriculum. Everything else in the academy exists to support those efforts. Auxiliary services such as food service and bookstores, the fundraising and public relations functions, the student recruitment and student records offices, the financial and campus information technology departments, and the executive leadership all exist to provide support.

New programs may be proposed with very modest budget demands. At the proposal stage of a new program, its champions are often willing to take on additional duties as an uncompensated overload and to work within existing resources as much as possible.

But as one former president noted, "Pretty soon they need a staff person to handle the extra work, and that staff person needs an office with a desk, chair, computer, and a telephone, and then an assistant who needs an office with a desk, chair, computer, and a telephone." It is certainly important to count the direct costs of a proposed new program and to be as realistic as possible about the resources needed to sustain it.

It is more difficult to estimate the indirect costs of a program, and those anxious to get approval for a new program may minimize the impact on support budgets. Very few departments operate at maximum workload capacity. Most can shoehorn in a few extra tasks over the course of an average day. But any new program will have some impact on support areas. These can involve checks being generated, accounting data being tracked, library holdings being added, computer processing capacity and data storage being used, utilities being consumed, mail being handled, and so on.

When an institution has a fairly homogeneous set of programs, such as a variety of majors that are all offered in a traditional format at a single site, then detailed analysis of indirect costs may not be important other than ensuring that support areas are efficient and effective. But when nontraditional or graduate educational programs are added to a traditional undergraduate institution, or when the college develops an enterprise that does not exist to generate student credit hours, a system for equitably calculating and distributing indirect costs becomes more meaningful. Often commitments are made to various constituencies that one program will not subsidize the other, that each "tub will rest on its own bottom."

Accounting staff understand indirect costs and can develop appropriate models for distributing support costs to each primary program area. But discussion is often necessary to convince staff in each program area that it is fair and reasonable to assign indirect costs in calculating total costs, especially when a primary program may expect to retain any net budget surplus. Unless costs include both the direct and indirect resources that are utilized by a program, decision-makers cannot accurately evaluate the net revenue from that program.

Incentives

A common and pejorative joke about faculty members is that trying to work with them is like herding cats. For many reasons, faculty members tend to place high value on academic freedom, creativity, and personal autonomy. They tend to have a strong affiliation and commitment to their field of study. Academic departments compete for budget dollars and for staffing levels. One of the academic deans with whom I was privileged to serve did an impressive job, over several years, developing incentives to align faculty behavior with institutional goals.

First, the dean was effective in the budget process in finding savings opportunities and convincing other administrators to allow some of these savings to be set aside for discretionary academic funding. Some of these funds were awarded directly to academic departments to be used as the department chose. Others were set aside in an innovation fund for which proposals could be submitted.

The departmental funds were awarded based on the department's combined scores on several factors. Departments were awarded points for generating student credit hours, attracting student majors, raising class enrollment levels within parameters, reducing costs per student credit hour, and similar efficiency measures. Academic quality measures included faculty and student participation on-campus and off-campus in enrichment programs, publishing, and presentations. The dean also incorporated a "community citizenship" measure. Support departments were asked to rate the academic departments based on how the faculty treated support staff and used support services.

The innovation fund was used to provide an opportunity for faculty to develop pilot programs that they believed would ultimately attract additional students and become self-sustaining through the generation of increased net revenues. Innovation grants were made for periods of up to three years. These were a great encouragement to faculty creativity.

Concept Four: Meaningful Measurements

Each campus must determine which measurements are significant in identifying its quality, its direction of change, and its viability. Some areas of higher education, such as accounting and financial records and student enrollment figures, are governed by standardized definitions and reporting rules at the state and federal levels. In such areas, it is fairly straightforward to make comparisons among different colleges. Such comparisons are desirable for gaining insight into one's own effectiveness, strengths, and opportunities for improvement. Much of the standardized data, however, is at a highly aggregated level. Decision-makers need reliable data that is relevant to strategic decisions, at an appropriate level of detail.

There are some statistics that may be collected for one particular decision but may not be relevant year after year. There are some that are kept annually by all institutions because they have become accepted as standard. These may be required by various external agencies or be part of widespread voluntary survey instruments in higher education. The value of the latter is that comparative data across many institutions is readily available. Between these two categories will be statistics that are important at a specific institution, and these may vary from campus to campus. As an example, the following is a partial list of statistics kept annually that were important in my experience:

- The relationships in each semester and annually among student headcount, Full Time Equivalent (FTE) students (full-time student headcount plus one-third of part-time student headcount in a traditional program) and Financial Full Time Equivalent (FFTE) students (total tuition revenue divided by the annual full-time tuition charge per full-time student).
- Retention patterns from semester to semester by class (freshman, sophomore, junior, senior, and unclassified).
- Full-time staff equivalent numbers by academic and administrative departments including adjunct faculty and part-time staff.
- The average unfunded scholarship aid awarded annually per full-time student differentiated between new and continuing students.
- The annual unit value of the endowment and the number of units by general purpose (unrestricted, restricted for scholarships, restricted for faculty salaries, etc.)
- The percentage of total revenue contributed by each major revenue source and the percentage of expenditures by each major expense category.
- The percentage of alumni making gifts in each year by purpose and the average gift per donor.
- Student credit hours generated per term per Full Time Equivalent faculty, by academic department.
- Average class size by academic department.

Multi-year Trends vs. Data Points

Key statistics, calculated consistently over a period of years, are more helpful to decision-makers than single data points. Campus leadership should keep a fact book or other collection of annual statistics readily available. At least five years of data should be reviewed to discern trends, and ten years may be better. This is not to say that a single data point may not be a cause for concern. A significant drop in new students, for instance, calls for immediate review. But only in the context of several years of data can a single measurement be interpreted meaningfully and trends discerned.

The concepts of meaningful measurements and multi-year data sound basic and obvious, but their achievement is more problematic than might be expected. The ethos of higher education values personal freedom. There is much less standardization in this large and diverse service industry than in for-profit product industries. As key administrative personnel come and go, it is difficult to sustain consistent statistical reporting standards. Different administrators may have different preferences and priorities. An individual with prior experience on another campus may bring new data definitions and report formats with them. It is the responsibility of campus leadership to ensure that important statistics are defined clearly and retained consistently.

Additional Resources

Each of the above concepts is covered in much greater detail in a number of resources for those who want to delve deeper into a particular area. A good starting place for all business-related topics in higher education is the National Association of College and University Business Officers. They publish a monthly magazine with excellent articles and critical updates for college business officers, and they offer an extensive array of print and other resources.

CHAPTER FOUR

A Financial Primer for Higher Education

Lois J. Voigt

In concert with the previous chapter, this essay provides a more detailed description of college and university financials. Although more comprehensive and complex, the concepts provided here enable the reader increased opportunity for leading change in our increasingly complicated financial world.

Higher educational finances remain a mystery to most, including many college administrators and boards of trustees' members. This is due in part to the nature of higher education's funding sources resulting in financial reporting requirements that are far more complex than most for-profit entities. Therefore, the goal of this chapter is to introduce the tools, statements, and concepts utilized in higher education to enable the reader to be an informed participant in his or her institution's financial planning and assessment.[1]

The first two sections of this chapter are foundational to understanding higher educational finances, and use data from a group of small colleges to illustrate the concepts. The first section focuses on budgeting: ways budget data are organized and approaches for creating budgets. The second section briefly introduces the required external reporting statements, a source for available comparative data, and another used by governmental and credit agencies. In addition, this second section will cover the strategies used to assess the credit-worthiness and ongoing viability of an institution. The final two sections discuss key components of financial planning and key ratios used to assess institutional financial health.

Budgeting for Higher Education

There are three primary types of budgets in higher education: operating budgets (plans for annual revenue and expenses); capital budgets (new construction, renovations, and equipment purchases), and cash flow budgets used to track the cash status for a single building project, or for all anticipated institutional activities.[2]

Operating Budgets

The average administrator focuses the majority of his or her financial planning time and effort on operating budgets. This is because most are responsible for at least one department and because they summarize the annual financial priorities and influence outcomes of core institutional activities. This section addresses the primary components of operating budgets and presents several strategic planning issues related to them.

Operating Revenue

Most major types of revenue are presented similarly in both internal and external reports. Exhibit 1 below summarizes averages for the primary categories as reported to IPEDS[3] for the fiscal year ending in 2009 for a sample group of approximately 150 small, private institutions.

Exhibit 1 Total Revenues		
	FY09 Average	% of Total
Tuition and Fees	28,120,962	
Less: Financial Aid	(9,034,806)	
Net Tuition and Fees	19,086,156	55.1%
Governmental Appropriations	178,740	0.5%
Governmental Grants	1,958,790	5.7%
Private Gifts and Grants	4,113,143	11.9%
Investment Return[4]	2,033,089	5.9%
Auxiliary enterprises	6,240,619	18.0%
Other Sources	1,015,893	2.9%
Total Revenue	34,626,430	100.0%

Tuition and fee revenue is presented net of financial aid, that is, financial aid is shown as *reducing revenue* rather than as *adding to expense*. This reflects the long-term trend of increasing amounts of "unfunded aid," institutional aid awarded to students that is not provided from gifts or supported by endowments specified for that purpose. It represents revenue dollars that an institution never receives while "funded aid," on the other hand, is reported in either the *Private Gifts* or *Investment Return* categories. For this sample of 150 private higher educational institutions, nearly 90 percent of all the institutional aid is unfunded, and almost 30 percent of all "gross" tuition and fee revenue (the "sticker" price times the number of students) are simply dollars that arise from the differential pricing that results from the institutional financial aid process (see Exhibit 2).

Exhibit 2
Unfunded Financial Aid

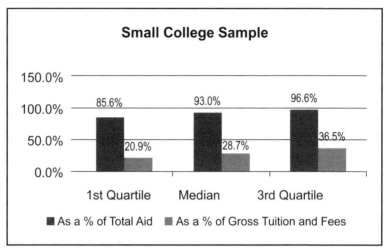

One may ask, "With such a high level of unfunded aid, why don't institutions simply reduce tuition?" Traditionally, high tuition signaled high quality. The utility of that reasoning has eroded in recent years as fewer than 10 percent of American families can now afford the average sticker price of a private institution, but several other reasons remain. The first is the need for most institutions to maximize net tuition revenue. Sophisticated modeling techniques have been developed to help financial aid staff at tuition-dependent institutions generate the highest possible net tuition revenue. The tuition "sticker" price is discounted by aid not only to produce the desired profile of an incoming class (i.e., academic quality), but also to improve net income by offering lower aid packages to profiles of students that research and history show are willing to pay a higher price, such as those geographically close to the institution or those with a certain income profile.

"Tuition dependency" is a term used to describe the percentage of income an institution receives from tuition and fees. High tuition dependency is viewed negatively because any change in demand, in students' ability to pay, or in governmental aid for students could significantly impair an institution's revenue stream. High tuition dependency, however, is the norm for most institutions, particularly those with modest endowments and gift revenue support. In the 2008 fiscal year, tuition and related fees as a percentage of overall revenue for private institutions was 65 percent,[5] and if one adds student revenue from *Auxiliary Enterprises* (dining, residence hall, and bookstore sales), total student fee revenue for many private institutions exceeds 80 percent. Thus, the decline in family income in the recent recession meant many private institutions' revenue from students declined (net of institutional aid), as did gift revenue and endowment investments.

The majority of private institutions receive no direct revenue from *Governmental Appropriations*, and *Governmental Grants* appear to be a fairly modest source of revenue at 5.7 percent in this sample (see Exhibit 1). However, those figures do not include "pass-through" aid: aid largely based on financial need (such as Pell grants) for which the institution acts as an administrative conduit for aid credited to its students' account balances based on governmentally prescribed formulas. Therefore, standard accounting practices mask the degree to which most private higher education institutions are dependent on governmental aid. Governmental student grant aid flowing through these sample institutions exceeds an average of $4 million or more than 20 percent of net tuition revenue. Beyond grants, aid in the form of subsidized federal loan programs can equal 100–200 percent of that figure, and unsubsidized federal loan programs can account for even greater sums. It is difficult to predict the government action and response. However, it can be said with relative certainty that if the economic recovery continues at a slow pace or falters, the implications for higher education and its students and families could be staggering.

The final consideration regarding operating revenue is that of endowment spending. Most boards of trustees establish an *endowment spending rate rule* to attempt to "smooth" the dollars spent from endowment investments from year-to-year. The one most frequently used is based on a percentage of the value of the endowment the preceding three or five years, although as Exhibit 3 demonstrates, even ten-year average rates of returns can be highly volatile. Most try to spend a percentage (often around 5 percent) that creates *intergenerational neutrality*: a percentage sufficiently low that excess earnings will cover inflation in subsequent years, but not so high that current year's students have to pay high fees simply because of an ultra-conservative approach to planning.

Exhibit 3 U.S. College Endowments					
Average Rates of Return for Selected 10-Year Periods Ending:					
	2002	2004	2006	2008	2010
Nominal Endowment Return (Median)	9.6%	9.9%	8.7%	6.3%	3.2%
Consumer Price Index (CPI-U)	4.0%	2.5%	2.6%	3.4%	2.8%
Real Rate of Return (Return less inflation)	5.6%	7.4%	6.1%	2.9%	0.4%
Source: NACUBO Endowment Studies (http://www.nacubo.org/Research/NACUBO_ Endowment_Study/Public_NCSE_Tables_.html)					

Spending rate policies are often questioned during times of extreme investment returns. In the late 1990s, many endowments were under pressure to raise their spending rates just before several years of negative returns, and in 2008, even as the ten-year real rate of return (returns less inflation) was falling to 2.9 percent from 6.1 percent just two years earlier, Congress was threatening legislation to force large university endowments to increase their spending rates. Only two years later, the ten-year real rate of return average had dropped to just 0.4 percent, which could suggest endowments should be spending almost nothing. At moments like that, campus leaders need to maintain the discipline of a long-term view and guard against both extreme optimism and extreme pessimism. In summary, slightly less than 75 percent of total revenue from the four-year institutions in Exhibit 1 came from student sources, 17 percent from current gifts and investment revenue generated from past gifts, 6 percent from governmental grants and 3 percent from other sources. In reality, however, students can afford to attend private institutions only because of a significantly larger tapestry of state and federal grant and loan programs that are in jeopardy in the current budget crisis.

Operating Expenses

Operating expenses can be organized in at least three different ways, and most modern financial systems can generate the same budget in all three ways. *Natural category* (or object code) budgets organize information by expenditure types such as salaries, benefits, supplies, utilities, and other operating expenses. This organizational scheme answers the question "What are we buying?"[6] and offers a simple way to model successive years' expenses by applying projected inflation factors to the key categories. Building a budget utilizing *only* this type of organization is not particularly strategic, but because colleges often link compensation increases to benchmarked averages, and compensation usually constitutes more than half of all operating expenses, it can be a fairly effective tool for budget-building, especially during times when institutional size does not vary and priorities are relatively static.

Exhibit 4 illustrates how a budget might be constructed using natural categories. Projected increases may be estimated based on a variety of goals and inflation rates. Moreover, some categories might receive differential changes based on projected changes in enrollment (i.e., faculty salaries) while others such as depreciation and interest could remain static until full-time equivalent enrollment (FTE) changes are so significant they dictate the need to sell or acquire new buildings.

Exhibit 4 **Operating Expenses by Natural Category**							
	FY09 Average	% of Total	$ / FTE	Inflation Factor	FTE Adjustment	Proposed Budget
Salaries and Wages	$13,134,868	40.8%	$8,630	3.0%	0.5%	$13,596,559
Benefits	$3,436,352	10.7%	$2,258	4.0%	0.5%	$3,591,675
Total Compensation	$16,571,220	51.4%	$10,888	3.2%	0.5%	$17,188,234
Depreciation	$2,242,474	7.0%	$1,473			$2,242,474
Interest Expense	$941,660	2.9%	$619			$941,660
Other Expenses	$12,476,006	38.7%	$8,197	2.5%	0.5%	$12,851,846
Total Expenses	**$32,231,363**	**100.0%**	**$21,177**	**2.6%**	**0.45%**	**$33,223,794**

"Functional (or program) category" budgets focus more on the question of "What are we trying to do?"[7] or "Where do we need to prioritize additional resources?" The functional categories reported to IPEDS include Instruction, Research, Academic Support, Public Service, Student Services, Institutional, and Auxiliary Enterprises.[8] Functional categories at the institutional level are further subdivided by one or more additional layers (for instance, within instruction, one might have graduate and undergraduate programs, each of those subdivided into programs in the sciences, then biology, chemistry, et cetera). Budgets organized by functional categories might first apply standard increases by natural categories (salaries, benefits, et cetera), and then apply additional increases to program areas prioritized by the institution's strategic plan.

Exhibit 5 demonstrates functional category expenses using my sample of modestly financed private four-year colleges. Note that the full-time equivalent enrollment for this group of private colleges is only 1,500. Larger institutions will usually devote a greater share of their resources to instruction and research, and a smaller proportion to institutional support. Expenses for student services and auxiliary enterprises will be higher for institutions with large residential populations. And the degree to which small institutions appropriately segregate research and academic support expense varies significantly (so it may be necessary to combine instruction, research, and academic support to get appropriate comparisons of those categories).

Exhibit 5
Operating Expense by Functional Category

	FY09 Average	%	$ / FTE	Inflation Factor	FTE Adjustment	Proposed Budget
Instruction	$10,713,990	33.2%	$7,039	3.0%	0.5%	$11,090,587
Research	$243,830	0.8%	$160	4.0%		$253,583
Public Service	$365,765	1.1%	$240	3.0%		$376,738
Academic Support	$2,260,762	7.0%	$1,485	3.0%		$2,328,585
Student Service	$5,273,310	16.4%	$3,465	3.0%		$5,431,509
Institutional Support	$6,870,654	21.3%	$4,514	2.5%		$7,042,420
Auxiliary Enterprises	$4,972,900	15.4%	$3,267	3.0%	0.2%	$5,132,331
Other Expenses	$1,530,152	4.7%	$1,005	3.0%		$1,576,057
Total Expenses	$32,231,363	100.0%	$21,177			$33,231,810

"Responsibility center budget" presentations organize revenues and expenses along with allocated institutional overhead by department and school, meaning each academic department is credited with a pro-rated share of tuition revenue and assessed the cost of providing registrar, financial aid, student billing, facilities, and other services. It attempts to answer questions such as "Which departments are spending resources?" and "Which departments provide resources?"[9] It serves to build awareness of the costs of campus resources such as space and computing services,[10] but can create at least temporary inefficiencies if units establish their own internal services instead of using centralized ones, and it is a very data- and time-intensive process.[11]

Though relatively rare in its purest form at small institutions, responsibility center budgeting is often utilized to meet situational needs. For instance, when a new program is added, or decisions must be made among options for adding several programs, institutions with strong financial modeling abilities will compare the direct revenue and expenses (those that will be budgeted within the new department) along with estimates for the impact on indirect expenses or overhead, such as the allocated cost of the space required, institutional computing resources, unique equipment, and accounting and human resources services.

Operating Budget Methodologies

As implied in the preceding discussion of how budgets are organized, institutions utilize a variety of approaches for building operating budgets. One of the most typical and time-efficient techniques (though least strategic) is *incremental budgeting* (Exhibit 4 in the prior section demonstrates how one might be operationalized). It assumes that the budget as it currently exists was appropriately rationalized in the past, so incremental additions are made based on inflation and enrollment factors.

"Zero-based budgeting" (ZBB) represents the opposite extreme: every unit must analyze and justify every activity for future budget periods, and provide an assessment of costs, benefits, and alternative approaches which are evaluated and ranked at subsequent organizational levels. A process predicated on ZBB is so time-consuming, and the underlying assumption that all expenses can be changed on an annual basis so impractical (especially given commitments to tenured faculty), that implementation of the process is typically partial: budget managers may be given the assumption that 90% of the prior year's budget will be maintained, or functional areas or sub-sections of an institution may be required to use ZBB on a rotating-year basis.

"Formula budgeting" is primarily used within statewide public systems of higher education to distribute state funding, or to establish criteria for developing and evaluating state institutions' budget requests. The formula may be based on a variety of ratios, with separate amounts established for credit hours at multiple divisions (undergraduate, master's, doctoral), average teaching load, square footage of physical plant, and a variety of other relationships. Though seen less frequently at private institutions, subsets of the technique may be utilized to evaluate the need for new (or decreased) faculty positions or residence hall staffing.

"Responsibility center budgeting" (RCB), as explained in the previous section, has sometimes been referred to as "every tub on its own bottom" or profit center budgeting. Units are assigned their share of revenue and expenses directly generated, and share in or are charged indirect revenues and expenses. It is used primarily at large universities where identifying overhead costs is a significant priority for institutions with large federal research grant revenues. Central administration and budget managers can expend considerable energy re-evaluating and negotiating the various internal rates, so though very time-intensive, it helps educate managers about the cost of often ignored support functions and facility costs.

"Initiative-based budgeting" (IBB) is a technique used to develop funding resources for new initiatives and so typically focuses on a small subset of operating activities. It may be funded by requiring campus units to identify activities that can be reduced or eliminated to provide a source for new, higher priority initiatives; by a pool of new funds; or by net revenues generated by previous new initiatives.[12]

Institutions will often utilize combinations of two or more of these methods in a single operating budget cycle. Incremental budgeting is almost always present in some form. Many institutions use periodic program reviews as a more practical proxy for ZBB. My institution recently used ZBB to (re)establish standardized budgeting support for all athletic teams. We have utilized IBB in various ways over the past five years, and use aspects of RCB to evaluate new initiatives.

Capital Budgets

Capital budget processes and procedures vary considerably among and between campuses. Small, cash-strapped institutions may maintain informal wish-lists that are addressed only when dire needs can no longer be ignored; others may create specific budgets when major building projects are identified as a fund-raising priority; and still others will incorporate all capital needs into a comprehensive, long-range planning process.

"Capital expenditures" are cash outlays for fixed assets (land, buildings and equipment) that have an estimated useful life of more than one year. One of the holy grails of accounting practice—the desire to match revenue with the expenses that produce the revenue—spawned the concept of depreciation, the estimated decline over time in the value of a fixed asset. Depreciation is calculated using the original cost of an asset, divided by the expected useful life of the asset, and the one-year value of that equation is assessed as annual depreciation expense.[13] Thus outlays for capital purchases are typically called "expenditures" to differentiate them from the allocation of depreciation: the annual expense that recognizes the gradual decline in value of a capital asset.

If institutions "fund depreciation" it means they generate sufficient operating revenues to reserve (and use) cash equal to 100 percent of depreciation for capital replacement. In part because depreciation did not have to be reflected as an expense in external audited statements for not-for-profits until 1996, institutional practices about how or whether depreciation is reflected on internal operating budgets vary considerably. Some do not budget for any depreciation expense, but continue the older practice of budgeting for equipment and principal payments on debt[14] within their operating budget (rather than in capital and cash flow budgets). Others gradually include an increasing percentage of depreciation expense in their operating budget, and still others completed the process many years ago.[15] Regardless of the internal budgeting mechanisms used, it is important that institutions generate sufficient cash to renew and replace buildings and equipment on a timely basis.

Not-for-profits also fund capital expenditures using donations (though donations to replace existing equipment and renovate buildings are relatively rare) and by incurring or issuing debt. The latter adds to operating budget expenses in the form of annual interest payments, and subtracts from the cash available to fund depreciation because cash must be used to meet future debt principal payments. However, the use of tax-exempt debt can be an effective financial strategy, especially for funding new revenue-generating projects such as additional residence halls.

The ideal comprehensive, long-term capital budget marries the campus master plan, capital replacement schedules generated by accounting and/or facilities management departments, and departmental requests for new equipment and facilities with expected funding sources: depreciation funded by operations, donations, and debt funding. Much like operating budgets, reality is often some subset of the ideal.

Cash-Flow Budgets

Cash-flow budgets at small institutions, when they exist, remain primarily within the domain of the accounting or finance departments. Cash-flow problems can occur even at colleges with operating surpluses for any number of reasons: if there are unexpected problems with collecting tuition and fees; if a large pledge is not paid as expected in the midst of a major building project; if expected debt funding is delayed; or if investments in theoretically "liquid" accounts are suddenly frozen. The 2008 recession resulted in numerous publicized examples of all of these.

Cash flow budgets should forecast monthly or quarterly cash inflows and outflows from operating sources (i.e., student tuition receipts, salary expenses), from investing activities (the sale and purchase of property and investments), and from financing activities (the issuance of new debt, gifts for buildings and endowment, and principal payments on existing debt).

Institutions employ a variety of cash-flow management techniques. If the fiscal year starts on July 1st, but the majority of tuition and fee payments are not due until September, a college must either have cash available from prior year's surpluses to meet July and August salary operating expenses, borrow funds on a short-term basis to meet those payments, or entice (or demand) earlier payment of tuition and fees by offering a discount for early payment or a penalty for late payment. To manage cash flow problems arising from capital expenditures, institutions may establish policies that require a specified (large) percentage of debt or donation funding be available in cash prior to approval of large building projects and/ or establish a minimum dollar amount that must be maintained to meet unusual or unexpected capital needs.

Regardless of the techniques used, senior management must find some way to regularly communicate cash flow status to institutional stakeholders. I currently report cash flow details to my board's finance committee, and a one-page financial summary given to all board members includes a graph that compares cash-flow balances for each month of the current fiscal year with those of preceding years.

External Financial Statements

There are three external financial statements which every institution must issue on an annual basis that portray different aspects of an institution's financial activities and health. The Statement of Financial Position summarizes the institutional net worth at a given date in time; the Statement of Activities summarizes the income and expense activity that occurred during one year; and the Statement of Cash Flows summarizes the changes in an institution's cash during a one year period.[16]

Statement of Financial Position

The Statement of Financial Position (referred to as a balance sheet in for-profit entities) summarizes institutional "life-to-date" financial performance by organizing financial data into assets, liabilities, and net assets (the sum of the institution's net worth). The first section shows what an institution *owns* (assets), namely cash, investments, buildings, accounts receivable (funds owed by students or other creditors), and promises by donors for future gifts (see Exhibit 6).

Exhibit 6 Statement of Financial Position[17]	
For the Year ended June 30, 2009	
Assets	
Cash	3,300,000
Accounts receivable	600,000
Prepaid expenses	300,000
Investments	25,400,000
Property and equipment., net of depreciation	53,700,000
Total Assets	83,300,000
Liabilities	
Accounts payable	2,000,000
Deposits	600,000
Annuities payable	1,800,000
Long-term debt	26,600,000
Total Liabilities	31,000,000
Net Assets	
Unrestricted	28,200,000
Temporarily restricted	6,800,000
Permanently restricted	17,300,000
Total Net Assets	52,300,000
Total Liabilities and Net Assets	83,300,000

This asset section is followed by a liabilities section or what is *owed* to others: accounts payable (bills owed to vendors, credit card vendors), annuities payable (estimated amounts owed to donors who have deposited funds in return for income for life or a specified period of time), and bonds, mortgages, or other forms of debt.

The final section is the difference between the first two. It is titled "Net Assets" and represents the accounting calculation for the net worth of an institution. It has three sections: unrestricted, temporarily restricted, and permanently restricted, the latter two of which are categories for organizing financial data based on the types of restrictions donors place on their gifts. Organizations to which institutions owe money prefer to see unrestricted assets because the institution need not abrogate any promises to donors to use those assets to pay what is owed, and because it demonstrates ability to weather future annual deficits while still having the funds to repay debts. The institutions in the sample group illustrated in Exhibit 6 had slightly more than half of their net assets in the unrestricted category

Statement of Activities

Otherwise known as the income statement, this financial report summarizes an institution's financial performance during the course of one fiscal year. It must show activities by the three types of funds: unrestricted, temporarily restricted, and permanently restricted, but activities can be organized in numerous ways. The most commonly used format first presents operating revenues and income (and the net change) before summarizing non-operating activities (endowment income or losses in excess of spending for operations; endowment, trust, and capital gifts; and activities related to trust and annuity investments). It should be noted that, even though the average administrator and many trustees focus most of their financial energy on the unrestricted operating budget because those expenses represent the mission and operational focus of the institution, the largest source of increase in wealth usually occurs in the non-operating section (non-operating gifts and investment returns).

Statement of Cash Flow

The final statement presents one year's financial activity by summarizing the sources and uses of cash by three different categories (operating, investing, and financing). While the format of the statement can make it even more difficult than the first two for a non-financial individual to understand, the concepts it presents are important: *"Does the institution have sufficient cash flow to meet operating and capital needs, and how is the institution funding those needs?"* A college may have a small operating surplus, but if, in a given year, it agreed to fund a large number of extended payment plans for students, then operations may not generate sufficient cash to pay expenses. Similarly, if depreciation is not "funded" from operations or gifts over an extended period of time, an institution may have to issue debt to get sufficient cash to repair and/or replace buildings.

Key Components of Financial Planning

Traditional financial planning activities focus primarily on the institutional operating budget. This section briefly highlights key components of financial planning for both operating and capital budget planning that most institutions need to consider. It is offered as a review to reinforce previously covered concepts of highest importance and to fill some knowledge gaps in what is an overwhelming subject.

1) *Tuition, fee, room and board pricing:* As noted in the preceding discussion, revenue from student fees accounts for roughly three-fourths of the total revenue for most private institutions, so an appropriate and sustainable pricing structure is vital.

2) *Financial aid discount rate:* The financial aid discount rate is the average percentage of tuition and required fees subtracted from students' bills in the form of institutional

aid. Institutions will often set two or more targeted rates, such as one for new freshmen, one for transfers, and for all students combined. Unless, an institution implements a "bait and switch" approach to recruiting (where one offers a large aid package in the freshmen year, but yanks it away in subsequent years), it is important that financial models estimate the impact of a significant increase in freshmen aid packages on subsequent years' overall discount rates and the resulting net tuition and fee revenue.

3) *Focus of fundraising efforts:* Operating budgets often focus solely on unrestricted annual gifts (frequently called the *Annual Fund*). However, strategic financial planning must coordinate long-term needs for addressing annual operating, building, and equipment needs, and endowment goals with the capacity for gifts (the institution's donor giving potential and major donors' interests), to maximize the efficiency and utility of fund-raising efforts.

4) *Endowment fund-raising and spending rate:* There are a variety of techniques for calculating endowment spending rates, most of which attempt to "smooth" the dollars available from year-to-year to maintain a steady source of operating revenue. Each has its strengths and weaknesses. My recommendation, regardless of the technique used, is that administrations examine their institution's endowment longitudinally by comparing increases in values (including additions through gifts and transfers as a separate component of that increase) with increases in its operating expenses. If, at a minimum, endowment values are rising at a slower pace than operating expenses, it suggests either fund-raising efforts need to increase (unless operating gifts are making up the difference) or the spending rate should decline.

5) *Salary and benefit structure:* Benefit packages at higher educational institutions tend to be much stronger than those at most for-profit institutions, a significant issue in an era like the last decade where some benefit costs increased at rates twice that of inflation. That creates dual communication challenges for administration: communicating to board members the importance of maintaining competitive benefits, and communicating to employees the impossibility of maintaining inflationary wage increases and traditional levels of benefits without raising tuition and/or decreasing staffing. Effective strategic planning must wrestle with the long-term impact of the institution's salary and benefit structure.

6) *Student/faculty ratio* and *student/staff ratio:* The financial implications of increasing the student/faculty ratio (from, for instance, fourteen students per full-time equivalent faculty member to sixteen students) are both simple to understand and difficult to enact: at face value, such a change should result in a 12.5 percent decrease in cost of instructional staff. The reality, especially at small institutions with tenured faculty, is much more complex. The savings (or incremental cost, if trying to decrease the ratio) may be significantly less than 12.5 percent if only classes taught by adjunct faculty are eliminated (added). And if the institution does not decrease the curricular offerings by reducing the number of majors or the courses required for majors, the only way to realize the goal is to significantly increase the size of general education classes: those most frequently taught to freshmen and sophomores, who often need more, not less personal attention if they are to return for the next semester. Attempts to decrease the student/staff ratio are equally complex. Regardless of the

complexity, administrators need to understand the structures that drive those ratios and address those issues when contemplating changes.

7) *Projected inflation:* Most financial planning models must take into account the potential effect of inflation on future costs, and often incorporate multiple rates: one or more for utilities, employee raises, benefits, and library purchases, etc. The resulting mix of costs has generally increased at a rate of 1 to 1.5 percentage points more than that of the general CPI index (see http://www.commonfund.org/CommonfundInstitute/HEPI/ for HEPI, the Higher Education Price Index, currently calculated by the CommonFund).

8) *Capital renewal and addition planning:* Capital renewal and planning for new buildings must be considered from a long-term perspective, ideally at least ten years. It needs to combine (1) deferred maintenance and replacement plans from the facilities department; (2) current equipment and building needs; (3) anticipated changes in enrollment; (4) gift and grant funding opportunities; and (5) a review of financial ratios and external economic conditions to determine if future capital projects can or should be funded with debt.

9) *Unanticipated surplus:* Most finance officers do not like to use surpluses to fund future expenses. That is especially true of using a surplus—a one-time source of funding—to pay for raises or other ongoing, multi-year commitments to expenses. Large unplanned surpluses, especially those that arise from large unrestricted gifts and estates, are often used to meet deferred maintenance needs, to make up short-falls in campaigns for new buildings, or added to board-designated endowment, the latter because then the

one-time source of funds can provide ongoing income to meet future needs, including salary increases.

Key Financial Ratios

The concept of financial ratios is quite complex and not for the faint of heart, but this chapter would be incomplete without a cursory treatment of the topic. We will trust your judgment as to whether you enter this section. You will be in a position to impress and astound your CFO if you do!

There is no prescribed list of key financial ratios to which all institutions must subscribe. A weakness in one area (for instance a small endowment and/or net worth position) may be compensated for by strengths in other areas (a multi-year history of strong operating surpluses, or non-financial indicators such as strong enrollment demand statistics). In addition, there is no substitute for understanding the individual realities of one's own institution that may or may not be reflected in its financial statements. However, when assembling a list of key financial indicators, at a minimum, most institutions should choose one or two ratios that summarize each of the following areas:[18]

1) *Annual financial performance:* Private institutions report their annual operating performance in a variety of ways, and so while they are useful for internal longitudinal comparisons, they are less useful for external comparative purposes. Other annual financial performance indicators include:

   a. *Net Operating Revenues Ratio:* It is generally recommended that the increase or decrease in unrestricted net assets divided by operating expenses (essentially, the operating surplus) meet or exceed 2 percent—a higher amount if an institution needs to generate an unusual amount of cash to meet principal payments, and potentially lower if that is not the case and there is no deferred maintenance issue. However, this ratio may not be meaningful for comparative purposes if one has an unusual amount of board-designated endowment (because of the resulting swings in investment income).

b. *Return on Net Assets:* This is the percentage change in the net worth of the institution, influenced by the operating budget performance, non-operating gifts, and trust and endowment investment income. It is generally recommended that the long-term average return on net assets be 3 to 4 percent greater than inflation.

2) *Measures of liquidity:* Measures of liquidity estimate an institution's ability to weather the impact of (hopefully unusual) events such as catastrophic losses of buildings on the campus that may not be fully covered by insurance or a large pledge that is not paid as expected when a building is already under construction. Examples include:

a. *Primary reserve ratio:* This ratio divides expendable net assets (an estimate of how much cash could be generated in a short period of time, i.e., if one liquidated all unrestricted investments) by total expenses. It is recommended this ratio meet or exceed .40, which would mean an institution could cover about five months of expenses from its reserves.

b. *Viability ratio:* This ratio has the same denominator (expendable net assets), but divides it by plant-related debt such as mortgages and bonds payable, and so estimates the ability of an institution to pay its debt. A minimum ratio of 1.25 is recommended.

3) *Age of plant/capital renewal:* There are a number ways
to attempt to estimate the "age of plant" or how much
deferred maintenance an institution has, none of which is
strong enough to stand alone without specific knowledge
of a campus' capital assets. Measures and/or recommendations include:

a. *Age of facilities ratio:* The ratio calculated by dividing
total accumulated depreciation by annual depreciation has been used as a way to estimate how well or
poorly an institution is doing in keeping its buildings
and equipment in good shape. It is recommended that
number be less than fourteen, but variations may be
fine (if a campus has an unusually excellent annual
maintenance program or an unusually high level of
annual depreciation expense).

b. *Physical asset reinvestment ratio:* This ratio divides the
amount spent on buildings and equipment in one year
by annual depreciation expense. There is no recommended target, but if the long-term average is less
than one, it is a strong indicator that the campus is not
investing sufficient funds in its capital assets.

c. *Replacement value reinvestment ratio:* One standard
that avoids the weakness of the preceding two (the fact
they are based in historical costs) is the recommendation that institutions spend 2 percent of the e*stimated
replacement cost* of physical assets (usually available from
insurance appraisals) annually on replacement and
renewal projects (Jones, 2011). Campuses with unusually high levels of deferred maintenance will need to
exceed 2 percent while those with unusually new and/
or well-maintained campuses may be able to manage
with less.

4) *Debt ratios:* If an institution is contemplating borrowing for a new project, additional ratios such as the *debt burden ratio* and *debt service coverage* will also need to be reviewed.

A number of years ago, a large consulting firm and an auditing firm developed the Composite Financial Index (CFI) which combines several ratios listed above into one weighted average designed to create a single number that summarizes an institution's relative financial health. The federal government uses a slightly different methodology in calculating a composite number for determining if additional monitoring activities will be required for continued participation in federal financial aid programs. Both methodologies have strengths, but the primary weakness inherent in both is that a single year's economic climate (such as the one in 2008–2009) can result in significant swings in an institution's score that exceed the true underlying change in financial health. Calculating three- or five-year averages will smooth but not eliminate those effects.

At a minimum, financial ratios for an institution should include historical trend basis (five years or more of past history), plus three years or more of projected data. Comparing your institution's historical trends with those of peer institutions will identify whether your institution's positive or negative trends reflect those of like-institutions or your performance is unusually strong or weak. Board members and senior administration should agree on a relatively small number of financial ratios (i.e., 4–10) that in combination with other data from admissions, instructional areas, and operations will provide concise dashboard indicators of institutional performance.

Conclusion

There is no simple methodology or magic ratio that once completed or attained assures an institution that it has "arrived" at the shores of financial utopia. I have worked at four different higher educational institutions and observed many others of varying levels of wealth. None, even those I thought were "rolling in it," ever thought there were sufficient funds to do all of the good things their mission and their diverse employees dreamed of accomplishing. However, financial literacy and a well-crafted set of financial indicators can help key stakeholders understand the financial challenges and opportunities facing an institution and enable them to participate effectively in strategic planning processes.

Endnotes

1. This chapter is primarily written from the perspective of private higher educational institutions because of my personal expertise, the intended audience, and space considerations. I will allude to some of the differences between private and public institutions (for instance, external statement presentation content and style are governed by two different accounting bodies), but many of the financial concepts and practices are similar.

2. Kent John Chabotar, *Strategic Finance: Planning and Budgeting for Boards, Chief Executives, and Finance Officers* (Washington, DC: AGB Press, 2006).

3. IPEDS, the Integrated Postsecondary Education Data System, organizes the results of a variety of financial, enrollment, graduation, and staffing surveys that must be completed by all postsecondary institutions that participate in federal student financial aid programs. Unless otherwise noted, financial data in this chapter were compiled in May 2011 from the National Center for Education Statistics IPEDS website (http://nces.ed.gov/ipeds/) for the fiscal year ending in 2009 for private institutions in the 2005 Carnegie classification type "Baccalaureates—Diverse Fields" whose full-time equivalent enrollments are between 1,000 and 4,000. The average income, expense, and assets per student for this group of 150 institutions tend to be 25 percent lower than the average private institution, while public institutions spend 10–15 percent less than this sample group.

4. Investment income in fiscal 2009 was an unusually poor year, so to make this example more illustrative, I adjusted the investment income to one representative of a more typical year. Actual average investment income for these schools in FY09 was negative: ($4,726,686).

5. Sandy Baum and Jennifer Ma, "Trends in College Pricing," *The College Board.* (Accessed April 2011) http://trends.collegeboard.org/downloads/ College_Pricing_2010.pdf

6. Chabotar, *Strategic Finance*, 76.

7. Ibid., 74.

8. Auxiliary Enterprises are operations supported by non-tuition student fees such as residence halls, dining services and bookstore that are generally self-supporting or revenue generating. The average Auxiliaries margin (excess of revenue over expenses) in my sample group was 22 percent, but results varied widely with roughly 25 percent of institutions reporting losses (note that these IPEDS numbers include allocated shares of utilities, maintenance, debt, and depreciation).

9. Chabotar, *Strategic Finance*.

10. I recall hearing more than a decade ago, that after RCM was instituted at a major institution, a "crowded" university suddenly had the equivalent of

more than a million square feet of unoccupied space: once budget managers were assessed a square foot charge, the demand for space declined significantly.

11. Larry Goldstein, *College & University Budgeting: An Introduction for Faculty and Academic Administrators* (Washington, DC: National Association of College and University Business Officers, 2005).

12. Ibid.

13. Institutions establish standards for the estimated life of categories of assets aided by accounting and IRS schedules, but those practices vary from as few as 20 years for new buildings to as long as 50 years or more. Establishing unusually long lives will result in lower-than-average depreciation expense which will help give the appearance of annual surpluses on the *Statement of Activities*, but may not reflect the true cost cycle nor discipline the institution to "save" sufficiently to replace equipment or renovate buildings on a timely basis. Conversely, using unusually short lives will increase expenses and may make an institution appear (relative to its peers, or to accrediting bodies or credit-rating firms) as though the institution has operating deficits or slim operating margins.

14. Debt service payments are comprised of both interest and principal (much like an individual's mortgage payment). Interest is accounted for as an expense because it represents the cost of using a bank or bondholder's cash. Principal payments, however, are not recorded as an expense because the transaction simply exchanges an asset (cash) for an equivalent decline in a liability: when an institution (or an individual) makes a principal payment, cash declines, but so does the debt owed, so there is no change in net worth, and therefore no expense incurred.

15. Results from an informal list serve survey of the 100 member institutions of the Council for Christian Colleges and Universities conducted in July of 2011 suggest that approximately 60 percent of those institutions budget depreciation as an expense in their internal operating budgets, with a significant number having made the change within the past five years.

16. See John A. Mattie, John H. McCarthy, and Robert M. Turner, *Understanding Financial Statements: A Strategic Guide for Independent College & University Boards,* 2nd ed. (Washington, DC: AGB Press, 2008) for a more comprehensive discussion and presentation of higher educational financial statements.

17. Data available from IPEDS does not include all asset and liability details, so some of those numbers are estimates.

18. See Sealy Prager & Co. and BeringPoint, Inc., *Strategic Financial Analysis for Higher Education* 2005. Available at http://www.prager.com/ibanking/raihe6. pdf (accessed April 2011) and Michael K.Townsley, *The Small College Guide to Financial Health: Beating the Odds* (Washington, DC: National Association of College and University Officers, 2002) for additional guidance, details about how these ratios are calculated, and advice on the appropriate use of them.

Bibliography

Baum, Sandy and Jennifer Ma. "Trends in College Pricing." *The College Board.* (Accessed April 2011) http://trends.collegeboard.org/downloads/College_Pricing_2010.pdf

Biedeweg, Fredrick, Lynda Weisburg-Swanson, and Catherin Gardner. "Planning for Capital Reinvestment." *NACUBO Business Officer* 32 no. 6 (1998), 23–29.

Chabotar, Kent John. *Strategic Finance: Planning and Budgeting for Boards, Chief Executives, and Finance Officers.* Washington, DC: AGB Press, 2006.

Goldstein, Larry. *College & University Budgeting: An Introduction for Faculty and Academic Administrators.* Washington, DC: National Association of College and University Business Officers, 2005.

Jones, Dennis. "Board Budget Decisions: Protecting and Building Your Institution's Assets." *Trusteeship* 19 no. 1 (2011), 30–33.

Mattie, John A., John H. McCarthy, and Robert M. Turner. *Understanding Financial Statements: A Strategic Guide for Independent College & University Boards.* 2nd ed. Washington, DC: AGB Press, 2008.

Sealy Prager & Co., LLC, KPMG LLP and BeringPoint, Inc. *Strategic Financial Analysis for Higher Education 2005.* (Accessed April 2011) Available at http://www.prager.com/ibanking/raihe6.pdf

Tahey, Phil, Ron Salluzzo, Fred Prager, Lou Mezzina, and Chris Cowen. *Strategic Financial Analysis for Higher Education: Identifying, Measuring & Reporting Financial Risks.* 7th ed. Prager, Sealy & Co., LLC, and Attain LLC, 2010.

Townsley, Michael K. *The Small College Guide to Financial Health: Beating the Odds.* Washington, DC: National Association of College and University Business Officers, 2002.

SECTION III

PREPARING
FOR CHANGE

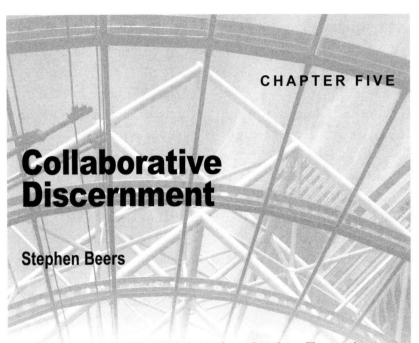

CHAPTER FIVE

Collaborative Discernment

Stephen Beers

The decision-making process is complicated at best. Tension between stakeholder's expectations, historical commitments, and recent financial woes all play into making a distinctive circumstance for higher education leaders. Gaining input from a variety of sources provides a leader invaluable insight and the opportunity for collaboration.

In challenging times, leadership questions arise that have no immediate or simple answers. Good solutions can sometimes rob an organization of the best solutions. Good ideas may lead to better ones; however, there is no yellow brick road that ensures a chosen trajectory is the right one. Collaborative discernment is needed.

Discernment provides a mixture of wisdom and intuition that can be applied to a difficult situation. Yet for people of faith, discernment is more than human ingenuity and insight. It is an intentional partnership with sacred wisdom and Spirit-filled guidance.

The pursuit of discernment is a pursuit of the wisdom and will of God. In the Old and New Testaments, discernment is depicted as something that provides direction in times of confusion and change. The writer of a prayer in 1 Kings 3:9a stated it this way: "Give your servant therefore an understanding mind to govern your people that I may discern between good and evil."

In addition, Scripture also speaks of the strength of working together. Solomon writes in Ecclesiastes, "Two are better than one, because they have a good return for their labor," and he continues by saying, "A cord of three strands is not quickly broken." There is strength in a multi-stranded, collaborative process where a variety of individuals provide synergistic wisdom and collective discernment. The collaborative wisdom fashioned by a council of voices provides an opportunity for a leadership team to see clearly the challenges and opportunities that lie ahead. These diverse voices provide a deeper and fuller opportunity for examining leadership opportunities, and, when appropriately managed, can assist with discernment.

The current challenges facing colleges and universities will require unique responses. Investing time and effort in collaborative discernment will return rich dividends and undergird the best decisions. Inviting others into the decision-making process does not release institutional leaders from their responsibility. Instead, it provides a richness and breadth of understanding that elevates the potential for institutional follow-though and success. To that end, this chapter focuses on the need for collaboration and some important components of navigating the collaboration process.

The Need for a Tailored Institutional Solution

At their core, all colleges and universities educate students; however, the way in which each college or university goes about fulfilling its mission is as diverse as the locations in which they reside. Acknowledging the uniqueness of an institution's mission, student population, programs, location, and ethos, to name just a few, will influence the educational process and help create a more individualized institutional action plan.

The diversity in higher educational institutions has been a hallmark of its collective strength. This diversity is first recognized in the mission and the particular perspectives of each college or university. These perspectives are rooted in deep assumptions that permeate the institution and they shape the way faculty members teach and may be observed in a university's historical commitment to a particular systematic theology. Any leadership decisions must take into account these unique institutional aspects. For example, a historically pacifist institution may not be comfortable adding an ROTC program on their campus.

Beyond its mission and educational assumptions, leaders must also be sensitive to the student population that the institution has historically served. Student demographics will always influence institutional direction and resource allocation, for example, as teaching methodology and support services are different for the adult and traditional aged student. Furthermore, the institution's current and potential new student market demographics will influence change opportunities. Student head count, transfer population, average age of the student, gender, residential verses commuter populations, and ethnic and international diversity should all be factors in charting any new direction. For example, if an institution has a strong graduate program or a significant niche in the adult market, it will have different questions to ponder as it looks to the future.

The opportunities of leveraging institutional programs, whether curricular or co-curricular, are powerful tools for change. But like refitting one cog in a complex machine, a single alteration potentially impacts many areas. Simply adding a new sport in the athletic department may impact budgets, facilities, staffing, scholarships, insurance, conference play, student travel, and institutional culture, to name just a few. Any of these collateral aspects of a decision may appropriately negate the assumed positive return on the investment.

Furthermore, the distance to or influences of population centers, commuter options, perceived safety issues, and local or regional destination points all should be influences accounted for in the strategic decision-making process. For example, adding an on-campus housing unit to grow enrollment may not be a simple option due to city ordinances.

Moving away from the outward institutional differences, one must account for and evaluate how the institution's financial health impacts opportunities. Historical tuition net revenues, endowment, regional competition, debt loads, deferred maintenance, unfunded discount, faculty and staff salaries, and utility burdens are all unseen financial variables that will play a significant role in limiting or expanding leadership opportunities.

All of the diverse and numerous variables mentioned above will require ongoing and institution-specific discussions to generate the best strategies. To be universally prescriptive with a "one size fits all" directive or to attempt to apply a boilerplate answer to any institution's challenge is unwise. Instead, each institution needs to assess its particular variables and, with conviction that is directed by the mission, should review and maximize all available institutional resources for change.

The Need for Collaborative Discernment

The editors of this book chose "collaborative discernment" as a topic due to the diversity of private education and the strength of the collaborative process. Collaboration can be much more than mere co-laboring; we are using the term here to describe a process that collects critical information from various entities across campus to be used in setting a discerning course for an institution. This process is intended to fully embrace the diverse contributions of individuals and acknowledges the power of collective wisdom. The author also believes that this process provides more opportunity for post decision "buy-in" for those involved. Below are a few illustrative benefits of this type of collaborative work.

Valuing Employees

At most of our private institutions we tout the ideal that each person at the university is more than a number. This is illustrated in all of our brochures and publications as we communicate to the general public that this institutional value makes our distinctive college a better place. Collaboration is inclusive. It begins with the a priori assumption that people matter and what people think matters. We begin by honoring people though inclusion.

Wisdom in Diversity

A number of social scientists and influential writers have turned their research instruments and keyboards towards understanding how group decision-making, when done correctly, out performs individual leadership decisions. A good example of this research comes from *The Wisdom of Crowds*, by James Surowiecki, where he summarizes his findings by stating, "If you can assemble a diverse group of people who possess varying degrees of knowledge and insight, you're better off entrusting it with major decisions rather than leaving them in the hands of one or two people, no matter how smart those people are."[1] Surowieski goes on to argue that this inclusion of a wider range of people enables all participants to speak more freely and, in turn, generates a more robust list of potential solutions.[2] Collaboration has the potential to meet a leader's need to generate a diversity of potential solutions, and, if Surowieski is right, the wisdom of the group will generate a better conclusion.

Gaining an Accurate Picture

What leaders need is an accurate picture of the problem and how decisions will most likely impact the intricate workings of the institution. The interdependent components of our colleges and universities require that leaders collect as complete a picture as possible before moving the organization forward. Collaborative processes have a higher probability of developing a more complete picture. A classic illustration of this is the age-old parable about a group of blind individuals who are describing what an elephant might look like from the limited perspective of what they can touch. They each accurately describe their portion of the pachyderm, but it is not until they put all of the information together that they have an accurate understanding of an elephant. To be sure, the information collected will always be partially shrouded in personal perspective, but a good leader and a good process can begin to distinguish between perspective and reality.

Collecting better information also reduces the need for having to fill information gaps with assumptions. It is our human nature, when we lack information on a given subject to fill in the gaps with assumptions that complete the picture. What is most interesting is that we do so by infusing information that fits best with our preconceived notion of the situation. Take, for example, a situation where a college administrator believes that funds are missing from the budget. For this simple example, the administrator may construct multiple conclusions to the question of where the money went, such as: embezzlement, poor accounting, or simply sloppy filing. What is interesting is that our perspectives and previous experiences, when coupled with our limited access to information, generally lead us to an assumed conclusion that we begin to accept or even act upon. A collaborative decision-making process is more inclusive and thus has the potential to get more information to more people thus reducing the number of gaps. This process generates and projects a more accurate picture. In the end, with the reduction of informational gaps, a collaborative process provides more opportunity for people to develop trust in the process.

Opportunity for Healthy Conflict

The opportunity for conflict in the decision-making process may be initially heightened with the inclusion of a wider diversity of opinion. However, these leadership challenges are worth the effort as the process provides the rich soil for the diversity of thought that generates better alternatives. To manage this well, a leader will have to learn the art of conflict management and group facilitation. A full discussion of this issue is beyond the intention of this chapter, but the trade off of managing conflict due to the inclusion of the diversity of personalities and perspectives is compensated by a better leadership solution. Patrick Lencionni, in his well-read leadership text, purports that "Healthy conflict is actually a time saver."[3]

Collective Buy-in

Conventional wisdom suggests that individuals accept more readily a decision that they have helped to shape. This is one of the reasons a parent may ask for his or her family's input before a big purchase or a move to another town. The mother or father knows that this decision will have an impact on each family member. The wisdom here is that if everyone in the family is in agreement with the decision then they are less likely to resist the change later. The standard term for this is "buy-in." Collaboration for discernment does not ensure buy-in, but there is more opportunity for individuals to have shared in the construction of the solution and for individual concerns to be addressed, mitigated, or at least acknowledged.

Buy-in is a powerful leadership concept for keeping the organization motivated and fully implementing leadership decisions. But there is an important yet subtle difference between buy-in and consensus. Consensus in certain situations is simply an intellectual acknowledgement or acquiescence to a leader's decision. Many times the individuals impacted in a leadership decision may not feel as though they were given the opportunity to be fully heard, and, in the end, coalesce in order to avoid conflict and not slow down the process. In certain situations, this is all leaders can hope for. In contrast, the collaborative process has more potential for buy-in, as the individuals are invited participants and partners in generating solutions that address their concerns. Stephen Robbins and Timothy Judge put it this way: "groups lead to increased acceptance of a solution. Many decisions fail after the final choice is made because people don't accept the solution. Group members who participated in making a decision are likely to enthusiastically support the decision and encourage others to accept it."[4]

The Art of Collaboration

Skill in using collaboration as a tool to gain a better understanding of a situation and create a more discerning strategy can be developed. Below is a short list of some ingredients that will assist in establishing a collaborative environment for discernment.

The Invitation

If collaboration is as significant a leadership tool as claimed in this chapter and as other writers have suggested, then what are some of the components of good collaboration? The answer may be outlined in Jim Collins' statement: "First you begin with 'who,' rather than 'what,'. . . . great vision without great people is irrelevant."[5] Getting a broad-based, diverse mix of people at the table is critical. This task of "invitation" is difficult but may be the most important aspect of this process. The research would suggest that a "diverse group with varying degrees of knowledge and insight" works best.[6] This inclusion also provides opportunity to see ourselves and to understand those we work with and serve. This invitation, as Max DePree notes, works to reject exclusivity and embraces inclusion.[7]

Listening

After the invitation, the collaborative leader begins by listening. Great leaders who have taken the time to record their wisdom for us are surprisingly consistent on this simple concept: listen first. Stephen Covey puts it this way: "If I were to summarize in one sentence the single most important principle I have learned in the field of interpersonal relations, it would be this: Seek first to understand, then to be understood."[8] Robert Greenleaf, the father of the modern servant leadership movement, suggests: "I have a bias about this which suggests that only a true natural servant automatically responds to any problem by listening first."[9] The perspective of Steven Sample, the former president of USC, is resoundingly similar: "But contrarian leaders know it is better to listen first and talk later. And when they listen, they do so artfully."[10] Listening is where leadership begins. The leader will always, if needed, be able to give the summary statement or provide the final decision, but until she or he truly listens, the collaborative process is circumvented.

Honesty with Clear Communication

Leaders need to facilitate a collaborative discernment process that encourages honesty. People are honest when they have trust in each other and when they believe that their candid comments will not lead to reprisals. There must be rules or ethical guidelines governing what is said and how it is communicated, but ultimately leaders need to give permission for open dialogue. In addition, the leader must be clear that their sympathetic listening posture should not be construed as agreement.[11]

Inquiry verses Advocacy

A component of listening is asking good questions. Good questions produce clarity and in fact show good listening. Mental health counselors and journalist are trained in the skill of asking good questions because their craft is based on an accurate understanding of a person's message. A central component of asking good questions is differentiating between inquiry and advocacy. Inquiry questions and summary statements attempt to clarify, probe, or test a particular assumption or proposal. In contrast, an advocacy question or summary statement is overtly or covertly intended to stifle or redirect an assumption or proposal. To be sure, there will be a time for redirection, but in the early "listening" stages of a collaborative process, inquiry questions are needed because advocacy question squelch the healthy process.

Conclusion

There is an old adage that states "good people with good information will make good decisions." Every group has its own personality, much like each person. When and how a leader provides closure to the collaborative discernment process is a function of external and internal timing, significance of the decision, group functionality, and communication styles, to name just a few variables. The purpose of this chapter is to propose that a decision rendered with wise input from a group, especially the group that the decision will impact, is worth the extra effort in developing and facilitating the collaborative discernment process. DePree's comment, "the most effective contemporary management process is participative management," summarizes it all.[12]

Endnotes

1. James Surowiecki, *The Wisdom of Crowds* (New York: Anchor Books, 2005), 31.

2. Ibid., 39.

3. Patrick Lencioni, *The Five Dysfunctions of a Team* (San Francisco: Jossey-Bass, 2002), 203.

4. Stephen P. Robbins and Timothy A. Judge, *Organizational Management*, 12th edition (Upper Saddle River, NJ: Prentice Hall, 2007), 22–23.

5. Jim Collins, *Good to Great* (New York: Harper Business, 2001), 42.

6. Surowiecki, *The Wisdom of Crowds*, 31.

7. Max De Pree, *Leadership Is an Art* (New York: Dell Publishing, 1989), 66.

8. Stephen R. Covey, *The 7 Habits of Highly Effective People: Powerful Lessons in Personal Change* (New York: Simon and Schuster, 1989), 237.

9. Robert K. Greenleaf, *Servant Leadership: A Journey into the Nature of Legitimate Power and Greatness* (Mahwah, NJ: Paulist Press, 19991), 17.

10. Steven B. Sample, *The Contrarian's Guide to Leadership* (San Francisco: Jossey-Bass, 2002), 21.

11. Ibid., 29.

12. De Pree, *Leadership Is an Art*, 24.

CHAPTER SIX

Implementing an Institutional Mission while Navigating Change

Albert J. Myer

The challenges of the current financial crisis places enormous pressure on institutions to pursue short-term gains at the expense of staying fully committed to the mission. This chapter is a reminder that institutional leaders must stay true to the institution's mission.

Short-term vs. Long-term

For an institution that exists to serve a distinctive mission, there is frequently a tension between the long term and the short term. The tension exists in business and other enterprises, as well as in higher education. In business, for example, there can be a tension between cutting research and development to maximize quarterly profits in the short term and gaining long-term profits from having new products created and developed by lively R&D divisions. In higher education, there can be a tension between getting more students and faculty members from anywhere—without regard for their interest in an institution's mission—and the long-term interest in having a distinctive institutional niche and raison d'être.

A Time of Change

Our colleges and universities, as well as other institutions in our society—public and private—have suffered from the current recession. Staff people and programs have been cut. Student financial aid has not kept up with rising tuition costs and this has limited access to educational opportunities for some students. Donor giving has been affected by the recession.

To be sure, the current recession has also had a positive impact: There has been a wider appreciation for the value of college education for individual students and for the society at large. College graduates are seen as more likely to get available jobs. Nations with better-educated work forces are projected to be more competitive on the world market.

A challenging trend of recent decades actually antedates the recession: The public is increasingly asking for assessment and accountability. In earlier years, the value of college education was assumed. Then an assessment movement began in the early 1980s. Polls reflected greater public ambivalence about the value of a college education. People wanted to know whether for-profit and not-for-profit institutions were actually delivering what they promised. Government agencies and accrediting associations wanted a "culture of evidence" and hard data on learning outcomes.

Institutions found that the public ambivalence about the value of higher education meant that governmental regulation and requirements for reporting have increased. Public financial support for institutions and student aid have sometimes been threatened when governmental budgets needed to be cut. At the institutional level, even when good data on outcomes could be obtained, providing the data and making the case has taken time and staffing, and these have affected institutional budgets. Finally, some college costs, such as those for healthcare for employees and students, have risen faster than inflation, and the public is concerned that these costs are passed on to students in higher tuitions and fees.

An Institution's Mission

A college or university with a future needs to have a reason-for-being. It needs to know and say how it is like some other institutions and how it is different. A board representing a public or private institution should have, as one of its top priorities, clearly articulating the institution's mission.

A problem at many institutions is that the mission is not articulated clearly enough to guide necessary decision-making. An institution that says its mission is to "do good and oppose evil" can change its fundamental purposes radically while insisting that everything it is doing continues to be within the scope of its mission statement.

In organizational structures, it is appropriate that the board, with its greater distance from day-to-day operations, take the primary responsibility for focusing on the long-term interest of its institution. Board leaders do well, from time to time, to remind new and continuing members of their board of their responsibility in this regard.

Some boards have day-long or multi-day retreats off-campus to work with mission statement drafts prepared by board subcommittees. They need time apart from the usual board agenda to get perspective on matters important for the long-term future. The board needs to involve administrators, faculty members, and other stakeholders in the development of the institution's mission statement.

If an institution is sponsored by a church or other subgroup of the larger society, the board representing the sponsors will have to consider the expectations of the sponsoring group. If the institution is independent, its board will need to lead its external and internal constituents to a reasonable consensus on its institution's mission. Having a clear and useful mission statement affirmed by stakeholders is important as an institution tries to keep focused on its goals in challenging financial times.

Strategic Plans

In addition to having mission statements, institutions have found it helpful to have in-house planning documents that are more specific and more frequently revised. The documents should be upgraded every two or three years.

If the characteristics of students the institution wants to educate are not clear from the mission statement, they should be made clear in strategic planning documents. Deciding why a school exists, whom it is to serve and how, and the kinds of people it must employ to achieve its mission are not matters a board can delegate to others. Boards have no more important responsibilities than these.

The strategic planning documents are not public relations pieces. There is a difference between a soap advertisement designed by the marketing department for the public and a chemical formula for the soap prepared by the production department of a soap factory. Those most directly involved in the leadership of a college or university need in-house "chemical formulas" that can be useful for their day-by-day decisionmaking, not only "soap ads." The planning documents of an educational institution are board and staff documents, not marketing pieces.

After twenty-five years of experience as a faculty member and administrator, George Keller published a work in 1983 that has led the field in strategic planning.[1] Keller proposed strategic (as opposed to short-term or tactical) planning. He proposed identifying distinctive and advantageous programs and positions of an institution in its field, emphasizing and enhancing those areas of strength, and making the most of those distinctive strengths in the market. In difficult financial times, it is easiest to decrease all program budgets by the same percentages, rather than to make tough decisions on priorities, but good institutional strategic planning focuses on an institution's distinctive mission and uses institutional resources to further that mission.

Enrollments

Challenging financial times are most likely to cause "mission creep" or mission change in a college or university when an administration or a board believes that enrollment growth is a key to desired financial stability or strength.

Why do many administrators and board members believe that enrollment growth helps the bottom line? For several reasons:

- In the short term, when faculty contracts are issued in the spring and a few more students without big scholarships show up in September, the unexpected extra tuition income is welcomed and the enrollment increase is financially helpful. If, on the other hand, there are empty dormitory beds in the fall, the budget is tighter than planned.

- Faculty members tend to like enrollment increases in their departments because the increases allow them to get more colleagues and cover more academic sub-specialities; whether or not this is better for students, specialization is widely seen as desirable in the university model that is influential in American academia.

- There can be some economies of scale. When an institution has a president, increasing the enrollment may require an increase in the total number of administrators, but it doesn't require a second president.
- Donors and the public at large often view enrollment increases as indications that an institution is popular and desireable in the educational marketplace. (Institutions with fixed enrollments, such as those in the Ivy League, compete with one another in "selectivity"—the ratio of applicants to admissions. Essentially, this is a competition to see which institutions can get more students to apply and then turn them down.)

These widely held understandings are not necessarily the last word, however, especially for the long term. Indeed, a study of small colleges over a twenty-year period has shown that, on the average, the institutions with greater enrollment growth in a given year were *not* stronger financially in the subsequent ten years.[2] Administrators and board members need to reflect on the fact that some leading institutions with fixed enrollments are financially quite healthy.

A not-for-profit college is not like a hammer factory that makes a profit on each hammer sold. It is more like the manufacturer of wrenches whose selling prices are lower than their production costs. In a not-for-profit college or university, the student tuition doesn't cover costs. On average, colleges "lose" on each student. When they get more students, they have to spread the endowment earnings thinner or get more donors to cover the costs not covered by tuition. Administrators and board members who think like hammer makers and talk in terms of economies of scale frequently do not see the whole picture: Over the long term, enrollment increases do not usually lead to greater financial strength.

The data represent averages. Some colleges with excess capacities can accommodate more students without much additional cost. (Some have overbuilt in good times.) The problem is that almost everyone thinks that his or her college is an exception to the rule and that more students mean financial strength, whether or not this is the case. Board members used to for-profit enterprises have to learn to think in terms of an enterprise that loses on each "unit" (student) produced, and that can be challenging. They need to ask whether utilizing excess capacity in one area of their school's operations will actually involve adding longer-term costs in another area and whether their instituition is really an exception to the rule that enrollment increase is on the average not financially advantageous. Apart from the financial considerations, when a college loses sight of its long-term mission, and when a board encourages getting students whether or not they are interested in the school's mission, the school's reason-for-being can get lost in the process.

Faculty and Mission

A school cannot implement a distinctive mission without a faculty committed to the mission. The problem here is that most colleges and universities operate on a "selection" rather than a "search" model for faculty recruitment. They have the idea that "there are lots of good people out there"—when actually it depends on what one is looking for and when and whether one cares if the faculty prospects are committed to the mission. (For example, there is not a long list of African American Baptist Nobel Prize winners in physics, if that is what a Baptist university seeking diversity in its faculty would like.)

Years ago, many colleges did not have many development staff members in deferred giving—officers seeking estate interests and commitments among people whose gifts would not be realized for years or decades. Now the importance of working for long-term gifts is widely recognized.

The need for a staff office working at long-term faculty team building and cultivating relationships with faculty prospects who will not be needed until some point in the future is less widely recognized. Challenging financial times have sometimes underlined the importance of cultivating deferred gifts; they have less frequently shown the importance of locating administrative responsibility for working with departments in cultivating relationships with future faculty members committed to the mission and needed for the long term.

Staffing for deferred gifts takes funding in the short term, but it can provide for financial stability in the long term. Staffing for long-term faculty team-building and working with strong prospects when they are available can require some funding in the short-term, but, like deferred-giving staffing, it can provide for mission accomplishment in the long term.

A deferred giving officer does not advertise in the *Chronicle of Higher Education* and then contact a selection of those who reply. (A National Football League coach who tried to get quarterbacks this way would find himself at the bottom of the league!) An officer working actively with departments in long-term faculty team-building will be an active "searcher," not just a "selecter."

In his eight-year presidency at Princeton, Woodrow Wilson and his dean, Henry Burchard Fine, helped make their institution the major research university it is today. They recruited actively. They brought bright young scholars to the campus as "preceptors" and then chose the best of them for their longer-term faculty. As in the case of contacts with donors, today's Ivy League institutions do not just advertise in the *Chronicle* and expect leading faculty prospects to apply. They search for and court scholars who will help them fulfill their missions.

Documents for Outside Agencies

Earlier in this chapter, I noted the increased interest of the public in assessment and accountability. Colleges and universities report to accreditation agencies for "quality control." The self-study an institution prepares for the visit of an accrediting team typically begins with a chapter on the institution's mission. The visiting team then reviews the evidence that the institution is achieving its mission.

A strength of American higher education has been the recognition of the contributions of colleges and university with different and distinctive missions. The purpose of accreditation is not to destroy the diversity of American colleges and universities; the basic purpose of the accreditation process is to assure all concerned that colleges and universities are doing what they say they are setting out to do in their mission statements.

The board has a critically important role here: to provide for review of documents sent to outside agencies to assure that the documents represent appropriately the mission and strategic planning documents of the institution. The board can ask two or three board members to read the self-study documents and to bring any questions to the full board's attention.

Preparing the self-study documents for accrediting teams is a substantial task requiring time and expense on the part of faculty members and administrators. Sometimes final drafts are prepared under tight deadlines. If time for board review is not scheduled into the process from the start, it may be hard to plan.

"Mission creep" is less likely to occur and healthy accountability is more likely to be realized when a board has clearly articulated its institution's mission and what its institution tells outside accreditors and agencies is consistent with long-term mission documents and strategic plans.

A Concluding Word

Current financial challenges can best be met if a college or university takes the occasion to review its reason-for-being, to articulate this clearly, and to give priority attention to building on its distinctive strengths.

Endnotes

1. George Keller, *Academic Strategy: The Management Revolution in American Higher Education* (Baltimore: Johns Hopkins University Press, 1983).

2. Albert J. Meyer and David H. Sikkink, "What Does It Profit a College to Add More Students? The Relationship Between Enrollment Growth and Financial Strength," *Christian Higher Education* 3 no. 2 (2004), 97–113.

CHAPTER SEVEN

Making Difficult Decisions Gracefully

Paul Lowell Haines

Leadership decisions, by their very nature, will have a far-reaching impact on the organization. Understanding how to make these decisions with grace is an art. This chapter will focus on how leaders can stay true to their mission while implementing change with dignity.

From at least one perspective, leaders at Christian colleges and universities are often at a significant disadvantage in addressing tough times. Many have grown up in insular, faith-based environments that urge, indeed demand, dependency on the Lord, trust in his leadership, discerning God's will, praying through to answers, patience and long suffering, and loving and caring for one another—all important characteristics of the Christ-centered, biblically-focused life. Yet, those very same laudable spiritual goals,

117

when not kept in perspective, can quickly become confusing "baggage" that complicates good decision-making.

Decision-making in Tough Times

This is especially true during stressful times, such as these, when one is confronted with dwindling enrollments, declining endowment returns, reduced federal and state financial support, pressing facility and maintenance needs, and the necessity to constrict programs and to reduce staff. On the one hand, such times demand thoughtful but decisive leadership and decision-making. When institutional missions are at risk, lives are being disrupted, and continued existence becomes questionable, well-intentioned institutional leadership that becomes paralyzed, pacified, or confused by the misapplication or misinterpretation of spiritual principles and aspirations can be fatal to the Christian college.

On the other hand, the simple, disengaged willingness to make the hard decision is not the answer. Decisions to reduce salaries, to eliminate positions, to terminate employees, to close programs and campuses, or to change course or direction have real consequences for real people. Our institutions are living organisms made up of complex individuals with complex families, responsibilities, obligations, and problems. To those persons, decisions made in times of crisis can be devastating.

For the decisionmaker, and especially for the Christian decisionmaker, such life-altering consequences should have meaning and relevance. Yes, decisions must be made and should not be delayed or avoided. Yes, failing to make decisions can have significant and negative institutional consequences. But, the simple commitment to make the hard decision, without more, will result in managing crisis ineffectively and in a way that does not honor the Lord.

The challenge then is to confront very difficult, potentially mission-impacting times with the wisdom and decisiveness of Solomon, but the heart and love of the Good Shepherd. How do we exercise effective, prudent, and often difficult decision-making while demonstrating Christ's love and care for his people. To be sure, no one prescription will address every difficult situation, as the facts and circumstances of each situation will be unique, but a few observations from experience can be helpful in navigating the storm and meeting the challenge.

Accepting the Challenge with Confidence

Few leaders actually seek out and revel in managing crisis. There is little joy in making hard decisions that impact people in negative ways. Indeed, the mere prospect of such activities can be quite unnerving. It is not unusual, therefore, to see leaders tasked with confronting hard times respond with some level of hesitation and self-doubt.

For the Christian leader, however, difficult decisions can be made with the assurance that God knows and cares about our every need, that he will not test us beyond what we can handle, and that he will honor our efforts to honor him. Indeed, most Christian leaders believe that there is a serious spiritual dimension to their leadership responsibilities and that they, in effect, have a "divine appointment"—that God has placed them in a position of responsibility, very possibly, for just such a time as this. When the leader combines this basic spiritual belief with the knowledge that he or she was appointed to a position of responsibility because others have confidence in his or her ability to lead, a platform is provided from which the leader can act with an appropriate level of confidence, despite uncertain times.

Days of crisis require leadership that accepts the challenge, engages it, and approaches decision-making confidently.

Fortunately, the Christian college leader has a reservoir of strength far beyond his or her own means and is capable, with God's help, to manage crisis and to surmount extreme conditions. Confidence in one's own abilities and in an omnipotent and omniscient God is a perfect place to start the struggle.

Focusing on Mission

Good times in higher education often are characterized by surplus, experimentation, and expansion. When residence hall beds are full and enrollments are at capacity, tuition-driven schools can conduct daily operations without difficulty while, at the same time, establishing new schools, programs, and majors, hiring additional faculty and staff, and funding improvements to campus and to facilities.

Unfortunately, history confirms that good times also can be characterized as periods when less attention is given to institutional mission and purpose. In times of plenty, institutions can become "fat and happy," and the understanding of why they were created and exist can become confused. At such times, institutions become susceptible to "mission creep" or to "mission drift," as is evidenced by numerous examples of formerly faith-based institutions that now give only a nostalgic nod to their founding purpose.

For the leader confronting crisis, a casual treatment of mission forecasts trouble on the horizon. Indeed, effective confrontation of the many issues that face an institution in crisis requires both a clear understanding of and a commitment to the basic reason-for-being of an institution. Without that, the leader confronting crisis has no compass by which to determine direction or to make difficult decisions. Rather, he or she becomes much like the captain of a rudderless ship in a violent storm whose sole purpose is to keep the ship afloat rather than to navigate to a destination.

As an initial action step, then, the leader who faces institutional crisis should focus his or her attention, like a laser, on the stated mission of the institution. A deep understanding of that critical information will provide the road map for all that is to come.

Understanding Fiduciary Duty and the "Charge to Keep"

Trustees and officers of institutions of higher education serve as fiduciaries of their respective organizations. As such, they are held to a high standard of conduct in carrying out their responsibilities. Included in that standard of conduct is the legal obligation and duty to act in good faith and, in addition, *in the best interests of their institutions.*

For the leader of the Christian college, fiduciary duty can be viewed as a legal obligation that is complimentary to, and not inconsistent with, the leader's spiritual assignment. The Christian college is a unique equipping ministry that is actively involved in carrying out the Great Commission. Accordingly, most leaders of Christian colleges would attest to believing that their leadership responsibilities are, in the words of the great hymn writer Charles Wesley, a "charge to keep." For most leaders there is a sense of spiritual obligation and sacred trust that requires their dedication to the founding purposes of the institution and to decision-making that furthers those purposes. For the leader confronting crisis, however, the legal and personal consequences of decisions that must be made are especially significant. Leaders know that what they decide likely will cause disruption to the institution and the lives of its people. In light of such consequences, decision-making that, by law and by charge, should be institution-focused can easily become individual-focused. Indeed, because of the great personal consequences of many difficult decisions, it is natural for the leader to gravitate to the easier, less controversial decision, even though that decision may not be in the best, long-term interests of the institution. In so doing, however, the leader compromises his or her legal duty to the institution, and the Christian leader his charge.

It is this natural desire to take the easier road, to make the less controversial or less life-impacting decision that underscores the need for leaders confronting crisis to have a clear understanding of their fiduciary obligation and a clear sense of their spiritual charge. Crises demand that decisions be made, and the reality is that those decisions often will be difficult. Their decision-making, no matter how difficult, should focus on the best interests of the institution as a whole—concern for the individual, although relevant and important to such deliberations, must take a back seat. Any decision made to a lower standard falls short of the legal duty and spiritual charge to which they are subject.

Of course, for the Christian leader in particular, this objectively presented challenge regarding duty and charge becomes a significant hurdle to successful confrontation of crises. Although decision-making "in the best interests of the institution" certainly makes logical sense and has a rational basis, it can become an almost unbearably difficult and confused task when placed in the context of decisions that impact negatively the lives of God's people. Christian leaders are steeped in a faith that demands loving your brothers and sisters, carrying their burdens, and seeking their best interests. How does one reconcile the parable of the Good Samaritan, Christ's example of washing his disciples' feet, and, indeed, Christ's love as demonstrated on the cross, with telling a Christian faculty member that his or her tenured position has been terminated or academic program dropped from the curriculum? There is, obviously, no easy answer. But at such times of conflict, it is important for the Christian leader to be reminded that he or she has a fiduciary duty to observe and a charge to keep—and that his or her obligation in addressing crisis, as one invested with the authority of leadership, is first and foremost to the institution, not to the individual.

Striving for Dignity and Decency in Decision-making

Effective navigation of crisis certainly requires leadership that is confident and willing to act, actions that are consistent with organizational mission, and decision-making that furthers the best interests of the institution. These foundational understandings and actions, if implemented thoughtfully, will provide the basic framework necessary to address difficult times in the most effective way possible. But these understandings and actions alone do little, if anything, to answer the question of how one addresses crises "gracefully."

Difficult decisions result in disrupted lives, inflamed emotions, and misunderstandings at every turn. Leaders making those decisions likely will be disrespected, challenged, and, at times, vilified. In such an environment, how does the decision-maker act with "grace"? Is there a way to confront potentially harmful and hurtful situations with dignity and decency?

The answer, to be sure, requires an added dimension of leadership skill and personal commitment. It has little to do with "what" decisions are made. Indeed, in this context, it matters little whether the right or the wrong decisions are made. Rather, addressing difficult decisions gracefully has more to do with "how" decisions are made and implemented.

Operating with Integrity

Most would agree that, at a minimum, good leadership demands conducting oneself with integrity. A good leader must be a person who can be trusted and whose word has credibility. He or she must be worthy of confidence and must confront situations and people in a forthright and honest manner. For the Christian leader, in particular, operating with integrity is of special importance as Scripture demands honesty and right dealing with others.

123

In times of crisis, however, the goal of operating with integrity and, in particular, the goal of being recognized for operating with integrity, can be especially difficult to achieve. In such times, motivations are often questioned, secret agendas are typically assumed, and trust is scarce. Leaders themselves, despite their best efforts, will be misunderstood and their integrity challenged.

And yet, for the leader who desires to confront crisis successfully, acting with integrity is a foundational requirement for achieving that goal. Those individuals impacted by decision-making must, in the end, be able to trust those making decisions. Although it is unlikely that any decision made in a time of crisis will receive unanimous support, those impacted by decisions do need to have faith and confidence, to the extent possible under difficult circumstances, in the decision-maker. A leader who is trusted, and whose actions warrant that trust, is one who has the best opportunity to address difficult times effectively, and to do so with grace.

Addressing hard times with integrity will not make the pain go away or the pill any less difficult to swallow, but it will lay a solid foundation of honesty and right dealing on which unintended injury can be healed, bitterness and high emotions can be calmed, and disrupted lives can once again find peace and purpose. The decisionmaker's commitment to conducting himself or herself in a frank, straightforward, and honorable manner will constitute the first step in a "graceful" resolution to crisis.

Implementing Decisions in Good Faith

Once difficult decisions are made, the leader confronting crisis, by necessity, will need to implement those decisions. The implementation process, in turn, will present the leader with another opportunity to demonstrate decency, good will, and grace in hard times.

The leader will know that his or her decisions have disrupted numerous lives and that, for many, life will not be the same going forward. Whether it is the student who must leave the institution and friends she loves because the institution closes its doors or no longer offers her chosen major, or the terminated faculty member who must disrupt the lives of his family in pursuit of a new position, or the student athlete whose sport is dropped, the leader will know that decisions have real-life consequences and hardships for real people.

Good faith demands that an institution and its leaders do what they can, within the constraints of reason, financial ability, and institutional best interests, to lessen the burdens created by difficult decisions. Good faith may require assisting students and faculty in relocation, offering reasonable severance packages, providing professional references, creating alternative opportunities for education, making available counseling and other mental health support, and extending insurance benefits. In addition, Christian colleges may want to offer prayer support, spiritual counseling, financial assistance, and make efforts to address physical needs. Leaders seeking to address crisis in a graceful and honorable way will do all they can to acknowledge and address the personal difficulties their decisions have caused. In so doing, they act with honor and their efforts demonstrate care, concern, and, indeed, grace.

Seeking the Lord's Direction and Blessing

The decisions facing many leaders in higher education today are, to say the least, daunting. If one dissects each difficult situation, the complexities and emotions that are revealed can quickly suck the air out of any room. The reality is that, in many situations, the circumstances may be sufficiently dire to dramatically impact programs, persons, or even the survival of the institution.

Although the Christian leader is vulnerable to that same sense of being impotent and overwhelmed, he or she can look beyond personal resources to a different source of strength. The Christian

125

leader believes in a God who is ever-present, all powerful, and certainly capable of addressing institutional needs and changing economic conditions.

That being true, the Christian college leader who seeks to address crisis gracefully must undergird each and every effort to address difficult times with the desire to honor the Lord, seek his wisdom and discernment, and carry out his purposes. The Christian college has no reason for being if Christ is not involved, if his purposes are not the purposes of the institution, and if its educational programs do not honor and glorify him. It is imperative, therefore, for the Christian college leader facing crisis to start each day on his or her knees seeking the Lord's will and blessing with respect to decisions that must be made and circumstances that must be confronted. For the leader who seeks to address times of crisis in a manner that honors the Lord and cares for his people, there is no better place to start and end the effort than at his feet.

Concluding Thoughts

There are no easy answers to how one navigates times of crisis in higher education gracefully, just as there is no three-step process on how to fire someone and make them feel good about it. The problems are real, the options limited, the emotions raw, the angst justified, and the responsibilities heavy. The leader confronting such difficult times typically does so with limited experience, inadequate resources, little potential for progress, and high expectations for success. It is not unusual for the leader to feel as though he or she is floundering in rushing white water, struggling to keep his or her head above the surface, and gasping for just one more breath.

These observations above certainly are not intended to be a definitive checklist of how one addresses times of crisis in higher education successfully. They do, however, provide a foundation on which to build. The leader who accepts the daunting challenge with confidence in his or her abilities and in a God who will lead and direct, focuses on organizational mission and purpose, acts in the best interests of the institution, addresses decision-making with integrity, manages consequences in good faith, and seeks the Lord's direction and blessing through it all will be well down the road to addressing hard days in higher education with competence, with honor, and with grace.

CHAPTER EIGHT

Caring for the Culture, Protecting the People

Shirley A. Mullen

*Every leadership decision impacts the individuals who make up the orga-
nization. Some good decisions may have a short-term negative impact,
perceived or real, on the organization's people and its culture. This chapter discusses how institutions in change can work to lessen the negative
impact on its most important resource.*

I accepted the invitation to write this chapter not because I
have any special training or giftedness in mitigating the painful
personal and institutional impact of change, but because this topic
is so important. My reflections are from the trenches, not from
35,000 feet up, nor from the perspective of looking back on the past.
We are in the midst of major institutional change, negotiating the
uncharted territory in which we find ourselves step by step. We are
seeking to move forward with tempered boldness that avoids the
tempting perils of either reckless abandon or paralysis by too much

discussion. Circumstances pull us toward the former; academic habituation and our own institutional tradition toward the latter.

Thus, I am writing from what I see in this moment. A historian by training, I am more used to—and perhaps more comfortable— looking back on things. Some of what I say will stand the test of time; some will not. I am also writing from a particular place. No two institutions are exactly the same. You are invited to read what I have to say and decide if it applies to your institution. Perhaps that very sorting out process will lead you to insights that are more tailored to your situation than anything I have to suggest. That is at least my hope.

As Christian colleges and universities, we share in common a dual call to steward the institutions and to care for the people who have come into our hands in this moment, a moment when our institutions are more needed than ever in both the society and the church, but a moment that also presents us with unprecedented legal, political, economic, and cultural complexities. We also share the creative challenge of translating this common calling into the particular and concrete circumstances of our own educational con- stituencies—for wisdom and grace are particular to circumstances. I offer these reflections to you from my place in hopes that they can occasion productive insights and sustaining hope in your place.

A Brief Word about My Place

When Wall Street took a dive in the fall of 2008, our college was in the third year of a new administration, the first new adminis- tration in thirty years. The classic resounding mandate for change that invariably accompanies a new presidency after a long season of stable leadership had, by the third year, begun to wane. It is by then clear that not everyone who wants change wants the same change. And *any* change, no matter how much desired or needed, is painful. There are real and perceived winners and losers in any institutional change. The pain of change is certain and immediate. The gains are uncertain and farther off. As a historian who has seen this before in other times and places, I am fairly confident in claiming that our administrative transition has been fairly typical and thus fairly challenging.

The proverbial shockwaves of the general economy met a college community that was already strained and wearied by the effort of processing too much that was unfamiliar—new faces, new structures, new approaches to budgeting, new program initiatives, new assumptions, new questions—even though much of the new had been freely chosen by at least the majority of the community, and chosen in great hopefulness. The economic crisis of 2008 thus altered the external environment in which we were already processing change. It introduced unpredicted variables into our planning, sometimes hastening the pace at which decisions had to be made, sometimes narrowing options. The external crisis also increased the potential for suspicion and mistrust of colleagues and administrators, and intensified the deep longing to return to "normal"—back home where things were familiar and where we had honed our strategies for dealing with distasteful but predictable things that we could not avoid.

The faculty, staff, and students care deeply for each other as individuals and for the mission of the college. Intense venting at the "institution" and even at the administration co-exists with equally intense loyalty and commitment to the community and especially to the students. People come here, and for the most part, stay. It is their lives, their choices, and their commitments that have made this place flourish over the decades. It is their fears and hopes that must be acknowledged and addressed in this moment. If they are not, any success at addressing the economic challenges of our institutions will be a Pyrrhic victory. It is the commitment, trust, and passion of our faculties and staffs that carry the mission forward. They must flourish if the institutions are to flourish for the long haul.

Naming the Realities

I learned long ago that situations had to be faced before they can be changed. It is better, though often painful, to get the truth out on the table and into the light rather than to try to deal with situations that are only partially visible or vaguely understood. The first step toward caring for the culture of our institutions and nurturing the people is to acknowledge as best we can what is going on. It is the job of leaders to *name things accurately.* Once the leaders have taken the first step to do that, others in the community will help to refine the "seeing" and the "naming," especially if you invite that help. I will identify seven realities of this moment where I am. You may have different ones, or you may add others.

Change tests the community fabric, revealing where the threads are wearing thin and where the strength is

There is a certain calmness on the surface of any institution that comes when everyone knows the rules of the house—especially those unwritten rules, practices, and traditions that might not be visible to outsiders or to the casual reader of the handbook. Everyone knows how he or she fits within the structure and everyone plays their hand with predictable regularity. When change comes, especially when that change is mediated by those who are perceived to be outsiders, it becomes clear very quickly who welcomes the change and who does not. It becomes clear who felt safest in the old system and who is most threatened by the change. I am not at all suggesting that the discourse will take place in terms of fears or safety. Rather, the discussion is more likely to be around which members of the community truly understand the nature of the institution, and which members of the faculty truly have the best interest of the institution at heart. Philosophic arguments and considerations of interest get inextricably intertwined. Some will choose to be loyal to their vision of the institution even at the expense of the unity of the community. The challenge for the leaders is to recognize the fears and the grieving that attend any change and to acknowledge that reality without allowing it to tyrannize the decision-making process.

Scarcity strains the trust factor

It is all well and good to talk about institutional mission and even strategic planning when they are theoretical matters. Once we broach the topic of aligning resources to support mission and vision, the tone changes. Suddenly, the institution breaks up into all its special interest groups, each trying to make the case that its concerns are the most fundamental of all and the most critical for mission. I have yet to talk with a department on either the faculty or staff side of an institution that is not absolutely certain it needs more positions to carry out its responsibilities. On the one hand, this is all good. It is important that faculty and staff believe in what they do and believe that their work is critical—perhaps even more critical than the work of many others—to the wellbeing of the college. On the other hand, when this is the case, and the administration or even colleagues make decisions about priorities that do not seem to favor one's own department, the *prima facie* response can only be, "There must be some mistake. 'Those people' do not understand the role of my department. They must be the victim of bad advice or just plain incompetence." It is difficult in this moment to see that many resource decisions are truly "judgment calls." Good, reasonable, and intelligent people—all of whom care about the institution and its mission—can come to different conclusions on the matter at hand.

Painful and familiar predictability is often preferred to the uncertainties of change

When I read the book of Exodus earlier in life, I always wondered why the children of Israel, when wandering in the wilderness, would voice their complaints in terms of wanting to go back to Egypt. Didn't they know that they had been slaves in Egypt? How could they have forgotten so soon? I do not wonder any more. I think they behaved just like all human beings when they are dealing with a new situation—especially one that seems out of their control. As human beings, we have a marvelous, perhaps almost infinite, ability to adapt to situations, even rather terrible ones, as long as we have enough time. We find a coping strategy that preserves a measure of control and agency—and even a kind of empowerment—even in the worst of circumstances. As long as we know we can count on things staying the same, all is well. When change comes, the comfort and safety is gone.

This loss of safety is exacerbated in the current economic environment because so many variables shift from month-to-month—even day-to-day at certain times. Any administration that tries to plan and introduce a new "predictability" does so at their peril. Even though the faculty and staff may know rationally that the administration cannot control the economy (any more than they can control the coming of spring), the fear of uncertainty is so great that it is easier to blame the administration for waffling or refusing to reinstate a new predictability than to stand with the institution's leadership in sharing the challenge of confronting the new external realities.

It is critical at moments like this for the administration to identify in tangible ways with the pain that they are choosing for the community

Perhaps this goes without saying. But when budgets are being cut or salaries rolled back or frozen or benefits changed, the administration must take the lead in absorbing the impact of these decisions. For example, if salaries are to be adjusted, the leadership must opt to take a cut first.

Everyone will assume that some simple solution—and especially theirs—has been overlooked

If a leader has not already been appropriately humbled by life's circumstances by the time he or she gets into leadership, a moment like this one will complete that job. No matter what decision has been made, no matter how much effort has been put into explaining the challenges of a situation, or how many options have been considered along with the pros and cons of their implementation, one must expect a series of e-mails or messages suggesting that "the matter is really very simple." If you would just do this or that, all would be well. These suggestions can come from trustees, from faculty, from staff, from parents, from alumni, and sometimes from students. The hard thing in this moment is to realize that the individuals making these suggestions really are trying to help. The temptation is to be defensive—and to explain that, yes, we have already considered that option and ruled it out—which in most cases you have. Instead, one must find a gracious way to respond that invites the person into the challenge as a partner, affirming that his or her perspective was exactly the one that came up in such and such a meeting.

Change will be experienced as loss with all the accompanying signs and stages of grief

The more stable a community has been or perceived to have been, the more any change will be felt as a "dying" of sorts. The responses will parallel very closely the natural human responses to loss of any sort. There will be denial. There will be anger. There will be the desire to blame someone. There will finally be resignation. Finally, there will be, for most people, a willingness to re-engage in the institution in some new capacity. There is little point in arguing with people in the midst of this sense of loss. It is not primarily a cognitive matter. We must walk with them through it, much as we would accompany friends and family members in grief.

There are no painless solutions to this moment; the challenge is to choose one's pain carefully and strategically for the long-term good of the institution, its mission, and its people

This is a tough reality for any leadership team to accept. We are in our positions because we have had experience solving problems, or at least we are here because we want to solve problems. This is a very humbling moment. This is not the kind of problem that can be "solved" in the sense of being done with it. With very few exceptions, most institutions are dealing with very difficult choices— none of which are good. Furthermore, this is in an environment that is, itself, constantly changing. So, it is not as if one can make all the difficult decisions in one month or even in one year and then have the situation settled. The challenge in this moment is to prepare our communities for dealing with greater uncertainty as a way of life. It is more like trying to change a culture—more like creating a work of art than trying to solve a math problem.

Reckoning with the Challenges

As difficult as it may be to name the realities of the moment in your institution—especially in such a way that finds resonance with the majority of the people in the community—the greater difficulty is leading the institution in coming to terms with those challenges. Some of that can be done in large communal gatherings (e.g., state of the college dinners or special community-wide meetings), but some of this must be done case by case, department by department, as occasions require it. One must look for the teachable moments.

Find symbolic actions of good will that appropriately mitigate the pain

In this moment, look for small ways of showing the community that you as leaders know they are walking through difficult times. This might mean giving an extra day or even week of vacation to the staff, especially in those times when the faculty are off duty already. It may mean a token bonus at a holiday time. It may mean focusing energy on new and surprising ways of rewarding those faculty and staff who, day in and day out, are *not* the squeaky wheels. If your institution is not already a place well habituated in showing gratitude, this is a time to invite the practice to begin.

Spread the pain as equitably as possible

This is one of the most challenging aspects of this situation. By now, we all know that treating people fairly does not mean treating everyone the same. But the next step is harder. What does "fairness" mean in a college or university community where everyone is critical to the mission of the college, but everyone is not crucial in the same way? One must take into the account the different interests between older and younger faculty; between newer and longer-term faculty and staff; between full-time and part-time faculty and staff; between faculty and staff as bodies; between departments; and finally between the short-term and long-term interests of the institution. There are no easy or one-dimensional answers. On any given issue there will be members of the community who believe that there are obvious ways in which fairness would drive a decision one way. There will be others who believe with equal vehemence that fairness would drive the decision in the opposite direction. On these matters, the best a leader can do is try to understand the culture of the institution so that one knows what fault lines are out there (for example, is this a community that would assume a salary roll back would be done in a graduated way or by taking the same percentage from everyone?), and then to explain as best as possible how a particular decision is arrived at, along with appropriate openness about possibly thinking differently in the future.

Find language that communicates appropriate transparency amidst the complexity and that balances confidence with urgency
In moments of change, communication becomes more important than ever. We all know that. The question is how best to do that. Part of that challenge is choosing the place and time. Sometimes it is better to build on existing structures of communication. (For example, make a point of regularly visiting the staff cabinet or the department chair meetings, especially if that has not been a regular practice.) At certain points it can be helpful to call large special meetings of all faculty or all staff or both faculty and staff—though one must be careful not to do this *too* often. These should truly be "command performances" when they are called.

Part of the challenge is choosing how much to say. Not everyone needs—or wants—the same amount of information. Whatever is said needs to be on a trajectory of full transparency—but there may be room to share more or less, with the understanding that individuals who want more can ask further questions. (I would also add the caveat here that "transparency" does not mean sharing everything. There is room at the administrative level, as in our personal lives, for discretion and discernment about the level of disclosure that is appropriate at each moment. There are no hard and fast rules regarding what is appropriate. It can help to think about how much information is essential to ensure confidence in the institution. Or how much information is essential for each person to do his or her work well. There is a fine line between needing to know so as to have confidence in the institution and just wanting to know as a matter of curiosity.)

Finally, perhaps the most difficult challenge is to determine how to share in a way that builds a balance of institutional confidence coupled with urgency. On the one hand, too much focus on "the positive side" in this moment can come across as mockery or "administrative spin." On the other hand, too much talk of "crisis" can induce panic when that is perhaps not necessary. You know your own community. You know what reservoirs of trust are there or not there. You know whether hard news brings your community together or splinters it. Sometimes it helps simply to name this dilemma—though that can also have the ring of over analysis and abstraction, covering over the issue with too much talk. We need the wisdom of Solomon on this point.

Gain valuable input from the various sectors of the community, while not creating confusion about the decision-making process

If there is any confusion in your institution about governance, it will be magnified in this moment. The stakes are high for everyone. And fears are rampant that decisions will be made that affect "me" without "my input." In this moment it is valuable to find ways to get as much input as possible from both the standard sources within your institution and also perhaps from one-time invitations for input. (You may even want to offer an incentive for the best idea of the month for moving the college or university forward.) Prior to seeking input, it is also critical to clarify the role of that input. Few members of the community would want to trade places with the campus leaders in this moment (though there are often some who think they would) or to have the responsibility of making the decisions that need to be made, but they do want to know that they are heard. The more loyalty there is in the community toward the institution, the more important it is that all ideas have been heard. So, find ways to generate and hear good ideas, and keep expectations clear about how those ideas will function in the decision-making process.

Plan so that surprises come on the positive side rather than on the negative side, especially in the budget process

This is a lesson I had to learn the hard way. In some of the early budgets of my administration, I counted too much on certain things happening on the revenue side (especially one-time infusions of revenue such as the sale of a property) over which the college had little or no control. I did this in hopes of deferring or perhaps even avoiding altogether some of the difficult choices we would need to make on the expense side to balance the budget. At this point, I am a strong advocate of building a balanced operations budget. This forces greater honesty on everyone about how much money is "in the checkbook" and allows any one-time surprises to hasten the possibility of good things that were unexpected, rather than frustrate current expectations.

Ensure that the community is being cared for—even at the point where the administration may seem to be the cause of the problem
In one sense this is the point of this whole chapter, but it also needs to be stated as one of the particular challenges. In these moments, the natural or default position of those in an institution is to assume that someone must be at fault. The initial instinct typically will be for the community to cast about for a simple explanation—and most likely that will be the administration as a whole or the presidency in particular. This is much easier than coming to believe that the whole institution needs to think about things differently, and much easier than doing the hard work of sorting out the impact on the institution of the national or global economy. The administration, even at the moment when they may be the object of criticism, must at the same time be the most pro-active in assuring that those who are hurting are cared for. That is our responsibility. The challenge is to do this in a way that does not generate further cynicism. (For example, "Here they are making these terrible decisions and then pretending to care about the implications.") Sometimes this pro-activity can take the form of inviting one section of the community to care for another—so that the concern of the administration is

mediated indirectly. The administration may not get the credit—but that is not the point. The point is that the community be cared for.

Communicate in such a way that establishes credibility for what is happening and that invites community members to be agents rather than victims in this moment

This is a moment when faculty and staff really do want to understand the institution's finances. People who might not have cared five years ago to have a lesson in institutional finance, or even those who are usually very happy to let the administration do the leading as long as "my" world is left alone, may suddenly in this moment want to know that the institution really is making the very best decisions in face of the actual, available options. Bringing the community in on the various options that have been contemplated and sharing with them the advantages and disadvantages that were taken into account can be one way of alleviating the feeling that a decision has been "inflicted" on a community. It is also useful if there are places where it is appropriate to bring areas of the college into decisions that relate especially to those areas and allow them to make the choice rather than make decisions for them. We are so much better dealing with situations that we have in some sense chosen for ourselves—even if the choice has been the best of not-so-good options.

Welcoming the Opportunities

It has become almost a platitude during this economic downturn that "one should not waste a good crisis." I usually like to stay away from platitudes, but this is one worth noting. There are things that can be done in a moment of urgency that would otherwise be impossible—or at least take much longer. For those who take God's redemptive activity as more than a theological affirmation, this moment is a compelling invitation for divine grace to be at work.

Welcome this moment as a time to invite the community to a greater knowledge and awareness of the world of higher education
One of the strengths of many of our institutions is the number of longstanding faculty and staff whose identity is linked to our institution more than to their discipline and more than to higher education in the abstract. Though this is often a benefit, in moments like this, it can easily become a liability. Unless one is a regular reader of the *Chronicle of Higher Education* or a frequent speaker at conferences, it is easy to think that this moment of challenge is only happening to our own institution. Look for opportunities to do comparative analyses of your institution with other institutions, both in and outside the world of higher education. Just knowing that one is not alone is helpful. And knowing the challenges faced by other institutions can put the challenges of one's own place in perspective.

Invite everyone in the institution to be active rather than passive in moving the community forward
Take this moment to offer incentives of some sort to those who come up with good ideas that can be implemented—ideas that in one way or another reduce expenditures, increase revenue, or enable the community to more creatively and energetically meet the present challenges. This can be a moment when the community is more open to new ideas than during times when everyone assumes all is well.

Clarify the mission and calling of the community and of individual members within the community
In a moment of change, it is easy for individuals to lose a clear sense of mission. Partly this is a result of preoccupation with their own fears, worries, or irritations. But part of this is that nothing exposes missional fuzziness more than economic scarcity. As long as everyone is getting enough money to do the good things they think are

important, many faculty and staff are content to live with ambiguity or loose boundaries around the mission. When budgets are cut, or one part of the institution seems to be favored over another, mission suddenly becomes everyone's concern. Welcome this opportunity for animated engagement around the mission. Celebrate that, at this time, mission is more than an abstraction. In this moment, mission can become more alive than ever. In fact, nothing is more inspiring to me in these days than spending time with students or recent graduates. God, in his mercy, finds ways to ensure that our students have a life-changing experience even in the midst of changes at our institutions. We must rejoice in that, be encouraged by it, and above all, be grateful.

Explore new networks of partnership both within the institution and outside the institution

In this strange moment of both economic scarcity and higher expectations from educational institutions, partnerships become much more attractive and feasible than in times past. For one thing, everyone inside and outside higher education is looking for ways to create efficiency and market visibility. For another, partnerships can enhance the opportunities available to students (e.g., in terms of shared listing of courses; or partnerships with local businesses).

Above all, give benefit of doubt during this time to the fearful, disgruntled, and critical so that when we come back to some version of "normal," the bonds of graciousness and mutual respect have remained intact

During any time of anxiety and uncertainty, people say things or e-mail thoughts that do not reflect either their best or their settled opinions. They are processing, doing thought experiments, trying out ideas. We must give everyone the grace of not taking every word they say as their final word.

Conclusion

We have lived through a very privileged time in American higher education. That world is changing, both because of the economy and because of demography, changing markets for education around the world, and a hundred other factors in this fast moving interconnected world of the twenty-first century. While there is no going back to "normalcy," there is, in this moment, the opportunity to remind ourselves of the true source of our peace, stability, and confidence. If our job satisfaction or our comfort or our hope in the future of our institutions was grounded in earthly predictabilities, that security was false to start with. We are called, in this moment, to practice in our personal and institutional lives what we have always said we believed, that our peace, our joy, and our strength is in the Lord God Jehovah whose mercies are new each morning and whose faithfulness endures through all generations.

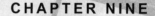

CHAPTER NINE

Critical Challenges, Critical Times

Timothy Herrmann

No decision is made in a vacuum—multiple variables are involved with moving forward. This final chapter highlights the interconnection between the current financial challenges and the ever-changing world of higher education.

That these are challenging times in higher education is unquestionable; however, the questions of what issues are most pressing and how they should be addressed are matters of considerable discussion and debate. Educational leaders, even within Christian higher education, are continually confronted with myriad microtrials that result from piloting complex programs and organizations within a milieu of quickly diminishing resources, shared values, and increasingly fewer commonly held beliefs and understandings.

As a result of these realities, every leader reading this chapter is faced with the necessity of forming and articulating—dare I say "selling"?—a shared vision to those whom they lead. Often this task is made more challenging by the many competing and conflicting views regarding the way that Christian higher education ought to be carried out. Nothing will be more important in the days ahead than for Christian colleges and universities to have a clear sense of "who they are" and a clear understanding that what they offer is unique in higher education, vital to the kingdom, beneficial to the public interest, and transformational to the individuals attending their institutions. These understandings must be a reality at two levels: of course in the basic philosophy and character of Christ-centered higher education, but also, perhaps more important to this discussion, as individual institutions. If these things are not understood, embraced, and communicated in our institutions, we have scant hope of surviving, or certainly thriving, in and through the considerable challenges confronting us. While virtually all Christian colleges display and recount worthy and inspiring mission statements, the *de facto* mission of many institutions seems to be merely to survive. While this may be understandable, simply working to "keep our heads above water" is unlikely to motivate the courage, dedication, innovation, and effort required to fuel the enterprise internally or to inspire the confidence of potential students, parents, donors, and many other external stakeholders upon whom we rely.

Articulate a Clear Purpose and a Focused Vision

The first challenge is to provide and articulate a clear purpose and a focused vision to those whom we lead. This process requires that we exercise the discipline necessary to avoid dissipating valuable energies and other critical resources pursuing initiatives and opportunities that are not central to the core. In challenging times we need the reminder that it is the essential starting point . It enables us to monitor our leadership practices to assure that in fact our actions and investments align with our stated mission and purposes.

The "follow-the-leader" behavior of many Christian colleges raises a number of questions about what really drives us. As a long-time observer of and participant in Christian higher education, I am left with the distinct impression that institutional leaders are much quicker to copy practices from other institutions that have been financially successful than they are from institutions that exhibit excellence in their educational practices. Of course, an institution can be excellent in both regards; but it seems that our penchant for imitation is far more compelling when it comes to what we perceive as a possible financial "lifesaver" than it is regarding the learning experiences of our students. While best practices in the financial realm are clearly important and a deep understanding of them must be a goal of all institutional leaders, it is also possible that certain financial practices and even potentially lucrative educational offer-ings may be inconsistent with our core purposes and values. When such opportunities present themselves, we are naturally tempted to apply a lower standard of scrutiny to our evaluation of their mission fit. Such temptations, though quite understandable in financially turbulent times, can have a potentially devastating Trojan Horse effect. What appears to be a wonderful gift may simply be the pack-aging for the very mechanism of our demise. When we succumb to a "close enough" standard regarding the mission fit of proposed initiatives and programs, we alter our institutional trajectory in a manner that could eventually make our stated mission and pur-poses irrelevant. When a proposal appears to have the potential of significant financial gain, it is much easier to gloss over issues of misalignment. Paul's warning to Timothy that "the love of money is a root of all kinds of evils" (1 Tim. 6:10 ESV) offers an important caution to institutions as well as to individuals.

Ironically, many evangelical colleges have gone to great lengths over the years to monitor and manage behavioral standards for students and employees, believing that the abandonment of such practices has proved the undoing of many schools that were once solidly Christian in their orientation. While such attention is legitimate, the lack of a strict standard in evaluating the mission fit of proposed programs and practices represents a far more ominous threat to our organizational health and heritage. We would do well to heed Marshall McLuhan's declaration that "the medium is the message" as we evaluate our priorities, especially as it relates to new, economically attractive opportunities.

For the remainder of this chapter, I will focus on some of the most pressing environmental issues that challenge Christian higher education today. Not the least of these is the current public perception of higher education. The 2006 U.S. Department of Education missive, *A Test of Leadership: Charting the Future of U.S. Higher Education*, declares that "among the vast and varied institutions that make up U.S. higher education, we have found much to applaud but also much that requires urgent reform."[1] This pronouncement sums up well the general feelings in this country toward the enterprise we serve. There is an acknowledgement that we certainly want and need higher education, but also a sense that something is wrong and must change.

Provide Evidence of the Accomplishment of the Basic Promises of the Academy

Although a list of the most serious problems would be long, the core concerns underlying most of the questions being posed by government, industry, students, their parents, and the general public can be captured by the words "cost" and "benefit." The skyrocketing cost of education is not a new issue; we have lived with it for many years. And while this is clearly among the most significant challenges facing educators, its scope and complexity go far beyond what would be possible to address here. However, what makes this issue of such particular concern right now is that it appears we have reached or are nearing a critical point. Costs have now touched levels which prevent many families from even being able to consider the benefits of paying the extra amount required for a private Christian education. Furthermore, even those who can still afford the expense, as well as the government, the general public, and employers hiring college graduates, are questioning whether or not the actual value is worth the cost.

The truism that "a high tide floats all ships" also works in reverse: "a low tide can ground the whole fleet!" In other words, the current national conversation regarding the state of higher education impacts us too. Although we may be convinced that we are part of the solution, this understanding is neither universally true of Christian higher education nor broadly accepted beyond. We must provide evidence to support our contention that Christian colleges and universities produce outcomes that are desirable and, in many cases, superior to many of our non-faith-based peers. We too are being asked to give evidence of our effectiveness to justify the high costs. If we really believe in what we are doing and believe that we are doing it well, this situation should be seen as more of an opportunity than a threat. Going beyond anecdotes to provide solid evidence of the excellence of our educational practices is both a stewardship responsibility and a powerful institutional witness within the academy.

While authentication of the efficacy of our efforts may not be easy to produce, one of the great hopes of Christian higher education is that we will come together to describe in a meaningful and evidence-based way how we deliver on the basic promises of the academy and how our approach to education is uniquely valuable, both to the individual and to the social fabric. While this, our second challenge, is no small task, it is surely one that demands our attention and that can provide great benefit to both our constituents and to those serving effectively within such colleges and universities.

Address Changes in the North American Mind

Because this chapter is primarily addressed to a North American audience, attention must be given to some ramifications of the incredible thought changes that have taken place in recent years. These changes have had so much impact on lifestyle and the way people view the world that they must be considered as we strategize about positioning and leading our institutions. In the current culture the postmodern and modern worldviews are struggling for ascendance. And while the shift away from modernism and toward postmodernism has been well-chronicled, it would be a mistake to think that the modernist perspective is not still broadly influential in our culture and particularly within the North American Church. Though a modernist perspective is no more "Christian" than postmodernism, many Christians seem more comfortable with it.

The point here is not to critique philosophy but rather to remind ourselves that these views strongly influence personal values and that personal values, in turn, strongly influence the perspective of parents and students regarding the nature, purposes, and benefits of Christian higher education. Equally important is the recognition that this reality does not just impact those outside looking in but also our own faculty and staff—the technical core that does the work of educating students.

It is obvious for those who spend significant time with "twenty- and thirty-something" employees that it is a new day. This group holds many new and different views regarding workplace norms, the boundaries between one's work and personal life, expectations of supervisors, opportunity for input into decision making, and even the nature of work itself. This observation is not intended to be derogatory—many of these differences, in fact, are healthy and refreshing. Rather, the point is that those who lead this generation of educators must take into account and, in many cases, accommodate these differences. The predominant view of the bureaucratic realities of the workplace and particularly of human resource administration is largely captured in the characterizations offered by *Dilbert* and more recently *The Office*. Although these younger employees can be forced to follow the rules (in fact in most cases they are quite compliant), such an approach will do little to capture their hearts, nurture their loyalty, or inspire their efforts. Remembering that "love prompts more than the law demands," while always wise, is essential in the current workplace.

Another ramification of these changes in thinking is that we have become an increasingly self-indulgent culture. In such a culture it is growing more and more difficult to make the case that the largely intangible, long-term benefits of a life or financial investment in an expensive, private, Christian education outweigh the more immediate gratification offered by a materialistic lifestyle. This trend increases our temptation to embrace a consumer orientation toward education. But this temptation must be resisted—a consumer approach is dissonant with Christian education. While students are consumers in certain aspects, giving in to this as a guiding paradigm encourages the view that education is a commodity. The embrace of this perspective makes it impossible to nurture, guide, and particularly challenge students in the manner necessary for education to be truly transformational. Postmodern thinking may lead students to question whether one can really even know that one educational choice is more valuable than another. This outlook combines with our lack of clarity regarding the benefits of higher education to create a "perfect storm" of uncertainty. This uncertainty is unlikely to reinforce the sense that Christian higher education is the best option available. As Gordon Winston reminded us many years ago:

> To a remarkable extent, people simply don't know what they're buying. And they can't find out until long after the fact . . . . For an investment in higher education, the outcome can't be known for 20 to 30 years, if then, and, if that weren't problem enough, it's a once-in-a-lifetime decision that can't be corrected next time around ("I went to Harvard the first time, but frankly it wasn't worth it, so I'll get my next undergraduate education at University of Montana") and it's a decision that people often make protectively on behalf of their beloved children . . . . Buying a college education is more like buying a cancer cure than a car or a house. There's a strong tendency to avoid regret and play it safe and buy what everyone considers "the best," if you can afford it.[2]

In such times it is important to keep in mind that higher education, and especially Christian higher education, operates in a "trust market." In other words, people send us their children and their money (very large sums of money) for a diploma from our institution because they trust us when we tell them that it is worth the cost. At the point that this trust is diminished or betrayed or that we offer a product whose traits do not align with the conceptions of worth held by our constituents, we devalue the very thing that we have to offer. In colloquial terms, "we kill the goose that lays the golden eggs." While no one does such things intentionally, we may do so inadvertently when we make curricular or pedagogical changes that compromise the broad understanding of our brand. For instance, Christian education is necessarily understood as "whole-person education." If this is true, curricular and pedagogical innovations that are perceived to diminish or to be "out of sync" with this focus may rightfully cause stakeholders to question whether or not there is truly enough additional "value added" to justify paying more to go to our colleges. In the understandable rush to develop new revenue streams, many institutions seem to forget the importance of market differentiation. In marketing terms, because Christian colleges and universities are unlikely to be able to establish themselves as low cost leaders, they are highly dependent upon their stakeholder's perception of high quality and offering a truly unique, even life-altering, education.

The preceding sections have discussed what could be considered foundational challenges or challenges which impact all of higher education but which have special significance or unique ramifications for Christian higher education. However, it is apparent that these are not the only trials facing college leaders. In the remainder of this chapter we turn our attention briefly to several other issues which, though not in this foundational category, must be given attention.

Managing Technological Change

An important element of the history of humankind is a recounting of the impact of new technologies. Technology has always had a significant influence on life and there has likely always been some level of resistance to technological change. However, it is safe to say that there has never been a time during which the rate and universal impact of technology has been so rapid. The speed at which new technologies are being introduced is truly mind-numbing. This reality impacts education in a multitude of ways, three of which I will address here: impact on budget, pedagogy, and communication.

The budget implications of technology are absolutely sweeping. Providing and maintaining basic technological resources for faculty, staff, and students is an immensely expensive proposition. Of course, the initial outlay required to purchase new hardware and software is huge but these costs pale in comparison to the costs of continual orientation, support, repair, and replacement. Thirty years ago information technology departments and staffs did not even exist; today they represent a large and growing share of the budget equation. When one considers the rising cost of education, for all of the benefits that it offers, technology has had a major negative impact. Although it can be argued that the increase of personal productivity offsets these costs, such an argument ignores the fact that for every secretary that has been eliminated by the increased capabilities offered by technology, we have added IT staff (generally at increased cost) to support the new technology.

Related to the issue of cost is the question of the appropriate adoption of pedagogical technology. Again, the rate at which new technologies and applications are introduced is incredible. Hardly a month goes by that faculty and instructional technology staff are not introduced to new technological teaching resources. Some of these offerings are presented so attractively that they are immediately assumed to provide learning benefits to students. But such is not always the case. Too often decision makers adopt technology without adequate evaluation, attention to ongoing support needs, plans for introduction and orientation, or long-term cost. It is not unusual to hear that significant technologies have been adopted without substantial input or evaluation from the actual teachers who use them. Also, leaders often forget to ask just how the adoption will directly impact students. One way students are impacted is when a new technology requires them to purchase new hardware or software. During a time of economic stress, the value of even a highly beneficial new technology must be considered in light of the resulting cost incurred by students. It is not just the overall price tag of our institutions that impact students, it is also what we often refer to as incidental expenses.

In a somewhat different but no less significant vein, the impact of technology on communication has been astounding. Whereas long-distance calls were once a rare occurrence generally saved for special needs and occasions, the advent of cell phones, essentially free long-distance, Skype, and Facetime allow inexpensive communication worldwide. Furthermore, text-based applications such as email, cell-phone texting, Twitter, Facebook, and others have changed the way we interact. While many of these applications provide tremendous benefits that we all enjoy, is it not also true that these new technologies assure that we are never out of reach of our students or their parents and they are never out of reach of one another? For all of the benefits that these connections afford, they also carry significant cost. We are usually far more adept at evaluating what new technologies will give us than we are at discerning what they will cost.

The impact of ubiquitous communication between students and their parents will be addressed in an upcoming section; but for a moment let us consider the impact on those who serve on our campuses. Who among us would not be thrilled to give up the daily barrage of emails? While many of the messages bring good news and glad tidings, many others are trivial or request information or assistance that could easily come from other places or be obtained in other ways. Although clearly much important work is done through email, it is also true that for most of us the constant disruption has an adverse impact on focused effort, productivity, attention, and, perhaps most importantly, uninterrupted thought. While this problem is much more than a campus issue, the exemplary campus leader will discern how best to help those they lead to deal with this modern reality. While on the surface the issue is technological, it is more likely to be solved by theology than technology. Thoughtful leaders who are willing and able to confront the disconnection between how we are made and how we currently do business will provide a great service to their institution, its students, and those who serve within.

Institutional Competition

The problem of escalating cost has been touched upon many times already. However, we would be remiss not to revisit it briefly one more time regarding the way it has impacted the interaction of sister institutions. While colleges and universities like ours have long competed with one another for students, it was a competition that was largely local, regional, or even denominational. But with the advent of online and other distance learning strategies, any sense of institutional "territory" has been removed. When considering program expansion, institutions seem to often ask the question "Can we?" rather than "Should we?" In the for-profit sector, the bottom line and accreditation concerns are the only limitation to growth strategies. Thus, if anticipated returns justify expansion, the corporation has an ethical responsibility to its shareholders to pursue profit. The responsibility of these institutions to make decisions on the basis of maximizing profit is what forces me to conclude that "for-profit" and "Christian" are incompatible partners in education.[3] Perhaps even more incongruent are those not-for-profit colleges and universities that use the advantage of their tax exempt status to operate in a for-profit, even predatory manner.

While good business practices are generally quite compatible with Christian educational ideals, this is not always the case. When there is an incongruence, Christian institutions have no choice but to faithfully serve Christian educational ideals. Paul House, discussing distance theological education, reasons that "it extends unsavory institutional competition to the world-wide web. We recruit students as consumers, and we treat sister [colleges] . . . as competing stores. We do it for the money."[4] If Christian higher education is to remain distinctive, its leaders will have to deal honestly and biblically with these philosophical-ethical issues. While wisdom dictates that we exercise pragmatism (practicality) in our day-to-day efforts, we must never adopt pragmatism as a guiding philosophy.

Emerging Adulthood and Increased Parental Involvement

The final matter of note is actually two separate but closely related issues. These issues are the phenomena of extended adolescence and increased parental involvement. The first has been characterized as emerging adulthood, and the second as helicopter parenting. Emerging adulthood is typically viewed as beginning at about age nineteen and extending to twenty-nine. Christian Smith, who has conducted a landmark study of the religious lives of this group, has characterized this as a period of "intense identity exploration, instability, a focus on the self, feeling in limbo or in transition or in between, and a sense of possibilities, opportunities, and unparalleled hope . . . often accompanied . . . by large doses of transience, confusion, anxiety, self-obsession, melodrama, conflict, disappointment, and sometimes emotional devastation."[5] Although it is unlikely the job of those reading this chapter to deal directly with student issues, these characteristics definitely do impact how students interact with our institutions. These characteristics influence the needs that students bring with them and the issues that must be addressed through various support and educational structures and programs. While it is unfair and unwise to assign a collective identity to any generation of students, some broad, observable characteristics of our current students are that they are less independent, require greater feedback, are more sensitive to criticism, and expect accommodation of their personal circumstances. And when you meet their parents you understand why!

Many of us have raised our children in this culture. As a result, it is very likely that we have unwittingly adopted parenting behaviors that characterize us too as helicopter parents. This may actually be a helpful reminder that such parents are not the enemy. In fact, many of them are just like us—parents who love their children and want them to be successful and happy. The irony is that while we crave the wellbeing of our children, over-involvement in their lives is more likely to demotivate them and actually prevent them from achieving the aspirations that we hold for them. Worse yet, over-involved parenting can negatively impact identity development and ultimately their ability to function as healthy, confident, and independent adults. The great paradox is that our fear of their failure may lead us to adopt attitudes and practices that virtually assure it. These issues notwithstanding, it is clear that over-involved parenting impacts parental expectations, our institutions, and particularly the way in which we interact with students and their parents.

The leadership task here is to establish an institutional ethos that communicates an understanding that parents can be tremendous allies in their sons' or daughters' education while at the same time communicating the expectation that they interact with the institution and its agents in a respectful, non-intrusive, and legal manner. To challenge the parents of students towards proper, healthy involvement in their lives while at the same time communicating an unwillingness to tolerate, accommodate, or overlook parental over-involvement requires a careful balancing act. But the effort is necessary. This challenge also requires us to guide those for whom we are responsible to meet students where they are: intellectually, socially, and spiritually. Educators should be both equipped to provide the educational scaffolding needed to help students learn and grow and empowered to challenge the parents towards proper, healthy involvement.

Many other issues and challenges could be addressed in this chapter: diversity, globalization, faculty productivity, balancing teaching and research, for example. The intention here has been to address the most critical needs using broad brushstrokes. As we know, one of the most important jobs of leaders is to absorb and process the never-ending stream of challenges that confront them. But if one is not careful, leadership can simply become an ongoing, repetitive reaction to the troubles that present themselves. When this happens it is difficult to attend to priorities or to act strategically. So it is critical for the leader to address these and other challenges in a manner that actually focuses attention on critical institutional priorities. Max DePree once wrote that "the first responsibility of a leader is to define reality."[6] While this can be done in a manipulative, self-serving manner, this is surely not what he was suggesting. Rather, he was encouraging leaders to use their knowledge and skill to identify and articulate significant organizational challenges and to frame them in a manner that underscores the values of the organization. Such challenges do not have to prevent us from accomplishing our purposes but can in fact be used to help highlight and accomplish those priorities.

In closing, let me offer a powerful prophetic word from T. S. Eliot's *Choruses from the Rock*:

The endless cycle of idea and action,
Endless invention, endless experiment,
Brings knowledge of motion, but not of stillness;
Knowledge of speech, but not of silence;
Knowledge of words, and ignorance of the Word.
All our knowledge brings us nearer to our ignorance,
All our ignorance brings us nearer to death,
But nearness to death no nearer to GOD.
Where is the Life we have lost in living?
Where is the wisdom we have lost in knowledge?
Where is the knowledge we have lost in information?
The cycles of Heaven in twenty centuries
Bring us farther from GOD and nearer to the Dust.[7]

As leaders in Christian higher education we have the opportunity to model for our students and colleagues what it means to engage in meaningful, God-centered effort. We can demonstrate how, by doing the work that we are called to, we can participate in bringing about, in ways large and small, a reality different than the one which Eliot decries. Even more significantly, we can help to shape our institutions into model learning communities that display for our students a different reality: one in which innovation recognizes the way God has created humankind; one which acknowledges the value of both silence and of the Word; one in which living brings us closer to Life; one in which knowledge is connected to wisdom; and, ultimately, one which moves us closer to, not farther from, God. So be it!

Endnotes

1. U. S. Department of Education, *A Test of Leadership: Charting the Future of U. S. Higher Education* (Washington, D.C., 2006), ix.

2. Gordon C. Winston, "Why Can't a College Be More Like a Firm," *Change* 29, no. 5 (1997): 33.

3. It is important to make a distinction here. This is not intended to imply that there are not many wonderful and committed Christians working within "for-profit" institutions, but rather that the author believes that the profit motive is incongruent with the aims and purposes of Christ-centered education.

4. Paul R. House, "Hewing to Scripture's Pattern: A Plea for Personal Theological Education," *Colloquy* 18, no. 2 (2010): 4.

5. Christian Smith with Patricia Snell, *Souls in Transition: The Religious & Spiritual Lives of Emerging Adults* (New York: Oxford University Press, 2009), 6.

6. Max De Pree. *Leadership Is an Art* (New York: Dell Publishing, 1989), 11.

7. Thomas Stearns Eliot, "Choruses from 'The Rock,'" in *The Complete Poems and Plays, 1909–1950* (New York: Houghton Mifflin Harcourt, 1971), 96, st. 1, lines 6–18.

CHAPTER TEN

Epilogue

Timothy Herrmann, Stephen Beers, and Paul Blezien

This final chapter is intended to accomplish two things: to highlight key themes from the preceding chapters and to challenge us to reflect on and think critically about our work and how our current perspectives guide us. As we (the three editors) wrote these words, we argued, disagreed, stood our ground, thought about uncomfortable ideas, and compromised. Clearly our abilities as educators were sharpened as a result of this process and it is our hope that you will similarly benefit as you wrestle with these ideas.

As you have "listened" to the voices of the contributors to this volume, surely you have noted an almost universal uneasiness regarding the double-edged sword of a volatile economic environment accompanied by rising costs to educate students. This is a troubling mixture even for the relatively few institutions with strong endowments. For those with more modest assets whose revenue structures are highly tuition dependent, this is an even more potentially deadly combination. The path to the future will be marked by those who develop a campus-wide financial sophistication and who collectively exercise sharply focused financial self-discipline. While the sacrificial accrual of monetary reserves along with a conservative approach to physical plant enhancement and resource allocation are not very exciting propositions, the first is always a wise choice and the second nearly always so. This new path will most certainly also include a requirement to sift through and test new opportunities that are grounded in the institutions' historical mission yet sensitive to the influences of our time.

Practically speaking, one of the critical components of the difficult task of prioritizing limited financial resources is retaining the centrality of the institutional mission and incorporating the goals of a strategic plan in the decision-making process. This requires a widespread awareness and understanding of the mission coupled with a well-organized and campus-wide adoption of the strategic plan. Attempting the process of institutional budgeting and prioritization without these two important guiding resources is like going on a difficult journey without a compass and map. You may move around a lot but you have little chance of reaching your destination. It is also quite likely that you will litter the path with lost and bewildered followers in the process.

In both setting direction and implementing the plan, an invitation to campus influencers to become informed and fully participating partners in achieving outcomes of the strategic plan becomes a leader's focus. The inclusion of others around the table will always be fraught with complications, but when collaboration is done well a collective ownership of difficult decisions will provide synergistic energy to move the organization forward.

Difficult decisions that directly or indirectly impact the campus community will be required. How an institution and its leaders handle such decisions and the people they impact will speak more loudly than any words uttered by those in power. Therefore, as leaders we must commit to navigating change in ways that acknowledge the sacrifices that our community members have made as well as those they will be asked to endure and/or embrace going forward.

In light of the task set before us all, the goal of this body of work was to help educational leaders "better understand the issues, more fully appreciate one another, and ultimately, embrace and engage in a collaborative process to manage change." Furthermore, "this collaborative process [must capitalize] on the collective wisdom, knowledge, and commitment present in our institutions" (p. 15). We have tried to engage in this process as we have shaped this book. Furthermore, as we have reviewed and analyzed the contributing essays, we believe that they both echo and highlight the wisdom of exercising *collaborative discernment* in the leadership of our institutions. This approach was reinforced through the research findings reported in Chapter Two. Here, the seasoned professionals interviewed uniformly expressed their strong belief in and commitment to embracing collaborative discernment to unify and lead our campus constituents.

The editors concur with those surveyed that a commitment to collaborative discernment may be among the most important elements in navigating change. Faithfully engaging the spirit and skillfully employing the practice of collaborative discernment appears to be integral to successful institutional budgeting within the guiding boundaries of effective stewardship of both fiscal and human resources. Therefore, collaborative decisions that further the mission of the institution are, in addition, simultaneously declaring the value of the people involved. Such an approach best serves our institutions, the formation of our students, the world, and ultimately the Kingdom of God.

A Sampling of Considerations

Though the use of a discount strategy will almost always be part of an institution's financial blueprint, depending upon consistent incremental increases in the discount rate is an unhealthy and unsustainable strategy. Besides being a short-term solution, there are ethical considerations that are far too often ignored. While the world may embrace the pragmatic benefits of "necessary evils," institutions whose purpose is to prepare students to participate more meaningfully in furthering God's Kingdom must evaluate their practices with a more intense level of scrutiny.

Perhaps the same point can be made regarding financial aid policies. While most of us bemoan the fact that our institutions are more and more out of reach of the students on the lower rungs of the socio-economic ladder, we must acknowledge that our shift from an emphasis on need to merit-based aid is at least a part of the problem. Therefore, while the clear educational benefits of "consumer input technology" (the recognition that students educate students) is a compelling and reasonable institutional concern, we err when we forget that economically and socially disadvantaged students are a critical component of the "greater good" we seek to serve. And no less are they a critical element of a fully-orbed understanding of the church universal—the intended beneficiary of our efforts.

Equally problematic but with perhaps somewhat less ethical baggage is the reality of continually escalating tuition costs. This problem is seldom addressed effectively because we tend to try to hold down costs in the least painful manner possible—through across-the-board reductions. While this may be the most palatable arrangement for the collegial-egalitarian organizations that we tend to be, it most often hampers the efforts of exemplary, mission-centric programs while throwing a lifeline to the ineffective or less-consequential efforts of weak programs or programs that are less essential to the accomplishment of the mission. While this may be helpful to the short-term morale of an institution, it is certainly does not enhance long-term organizational vitality. Furthermore, it is a *de facto* expression that the institution has priorities that supersede the accomplishment of its mission. The unwillingness to pursue the mission with relentless single-mindedness is as damaging to an organization as the harm done by resorting to means that are incongruent with institutional ends.

We acknowledge that the changing cultural and political landscape will continue to impact our efforts in the future. Whether it is simply in the form of having to provide more extensive remediation for students' theological, philosophical, moral, or educational deficits or whether it is figuring out how we will respond to the strings attached to federal or state student aid, we must be diligent, circumspect, and proactive in preparing for such changes. The threat that Christian colleges could lose federal funding because of religious values and practices is entirely real. Of course, in addition to contingency planning, one of the best defenses against such an eventuality is providing unmistakable evidence that our institutions' missions and activities serve the "greater good." The more we treat education as a private good and students as consumers and the more we operate in a manner that promotes education as a commodity, the less likely we will be to convince a watching world that we are "different" in a way that implies "value-added."

The voices that have weighed in on this conversation have also noted the significant challenges related to the changing nature, demand for, and utilization of technology. These challenges alone will require incredible resources and wisdom to confront. Though it would be naïve to think that these challenges will be "solved," they can and must be managed appropriately and effectively. Our ability to do this will have great financial, educational, and spiritual implications. Thus, it behooves us to do all that we can to move from a reactive to a proactive orientation in regard to these issues.

Finally, increased expectations and questions of accountability have also received consideration from our contributors. While the requirements that accompany these changes are, admittedly, burdensome, the emphasis on accountability and stewardship implicit in the Christian worldview means that Christian institutions should lead the way in modeling healthy and meaningful efforts to provide evidence of the fulfillment of our institutional objectives and core values. Though we may agree that some things we do are difficult to quantify, we must also acknowledge the reality that much of what we do can and should be measured, monitored, and evaluated. The resulting evidence should be a critical component of setting institutional priorities and will be a significant aid in the process of making difficult decisions in a way that preserves a genuine ethos of care.

Concluding Thoughts

This book is intended to serve as a backdrop for the many questions and challenges that require a response from contemporary educational leaders. We suggest that this work cannot even begin until we can provide a clear and compelling answer to the question: "What is the purpose of higher education?" Or more to the point in our circumstances: "What is the purpose of Christian higher education?" We not only have to understand "who we are" but also exhibit precision in the declaration of our purposes. And those purposes must be made crystal clear to those observing, particularly the students who are most directly impacted by our institutional and educational practices.

Earlier in this book we were reminded of T. S. Eliot's prophetic utterances and their implications suggesting that one of the great strengths of Christian higher education is that we have the moral and spiritual wherewithal to respond to impending challenges. Our work is intended to connect wisdom and knowledge in a manner that brings us and our world nearer to God. We know that Eliot's reflections were not a rejection of invention or experiment or speech or knowledge—they were an indictment of the meaninglessness of educational pursuits without a worthy end or purpose.

So again, we have to ponder: "What is the purpose of higher education?" or as Neil Postman asks: What is *The End of Education?*[1] Some would offer a utilitarian response to this question: the purpose of higher education is to prepare students for employability so that they can become productive citizens who can help fuel the economic engine—then they will be worth something. The other dominant narrative in our culture is that education (in and of itself) will bring us happiness and fulfillment. And, since "we are the center of the universe," what higher goal exists? In contrast, we suggest that Christian higher education offers a counter-narrative to these dominant cultural messages. Pope Benedict XVI addressed a group of faculty in Spain and had this to say about the encroachment of these utilitarian values upon the academy:

> You who, like myself, have had an experience of the university, and now are members of the teaching staff, surely are looking for something more lofty and capable of embracing the full measure of what it is to be human. We know that when mere utility and pure pragmatism become the principal criteria, much is lost and the results can be tragic: from the abuses associated with a science which acknowledges no limits beyond itself, to the political totalitarianism which easily arises when one eliminates any higher reference than the mere calculus of power. The authentic idea of the university, on the other hand, is precisely what saves us from this reductionist and curtailed vision of humanity.[2]

Nicholas Wolterstorff also wonderfully answers the question, "What is the purpose of higher education?" when he reminds us that we are *Educating for Shalom*.[3] While we might debate the best way to accomplish this, it is likely that we are on the same page regarding the ends—the purpose of Christian higher education is ultimately to bring glory to God and to better equip students to work towards the fulfillment of God's Kingdom.

Higher education is surely one of the greatest hopes for development and restoration that the world has to offer. Colleges and universities are places dedicated to thinking, learning, and growing—places that, in the words of Will Willimon, provide the time, space, observation, and conversation required for the slow, deliberate process of learning and development.[4] Colleges are also places that nurture curiosity and commitment; places that are intended to expose us to great and timeless ideas, events, and people; and places that open our eyes to the discovery of new truth and challenge us to build and embrace new knowledge. Could there be any greater privilege than to devote our lives to learning and to helping younger, less experienced learners do the same?

Actually there is. It is to do so knowing that the end of our learning is to better know, understand, and partner with the Author of Life and Creator of all good things.

We are humbled and grateful to co-labor with you in the pursuit of this noble vision.

Endnotes

1. Neil Postman, *The End of Education: Redefining the Value of School* (New York: Vintage Books, 1995).

2. "Pope Benedict to Professors: Spread the Truth," Vatican Radio, August 19, 2011 (http://www.oecumene.radiovaticana.org/en1/Articolo.asp?c=513651)

3. Nicholas Wolterstorff, Clarence W. Joldersma, and Gloria Goris Stronks, *Educating for Shalom: Essays on Christian Higher Education* (Grand Rapids, Mich.: Eerdmans, 2004).

4. William H. Willimon, "Religious Faith and the Development of Character on Campus," *Educational Record* 78 (1997): 73–79.

Contributors

Stephen Beers serves as the Vice-President for Student Development, Athletics, and Facilities at John Brown University. He also directs and teaches in the higher education masters program at JBU along with teaching undergraduate management courses. Steve is currently serving a two-year term as president of the Association for Christians in Student Development (ACSD). His other publications include *The Soul of the Christian University: A Field Guide for Educators* (ACU Press, 2008). Steve earned his BA from Taylor University, a MS from Wright State University, and an EdD from Ball State University.

Paul Blezien currently serves as the Senior Vice President of William Jessup University. He has been at WJU since 2004, has been on staff at Northwestern College (IA), and the University of Wisconsin. He has taught as an adjunct instructor in graduate education at Geneva College, Azusa Pacific University and the University of Sioux Falls. Paul received a BS from the University of Wisconsin at Stevens Point, MA from Ball State University, and an EdD from Azusa Pacific University.

Polly Graham is currently a Resident Director at Indiana Wesleyan University and serves as the technical editor for the Growth Journal. Polly earned a BS from Taylor University in English

Education and a MA also from Taylor in Student Development and Higher Education.

Patricia Gustavson is now retired and worked in Christian higher education for thirty-six years, the last twenty-four of which were at John Brown University as Vice President for Finance and Administration. She has served on boards and committees of the National Association of College and University Business Officers, the Southern Association of College and University Business Officers, the Council of Christian Colleges and Universities and the Association of Business Administrators of Christian Colleges. She holds an MBA from the University of Arkansas.

Paul Lowell Haines is a partner in the international law firm of Faegre Baker Daniels, where he has practiced for more than twenty years specializing in the law of tax exempt organizations (he leads the firm's Exempt Organizations Practice Group) and, more specifically, in the law of higher education. He provides legal counsel to dozens of colleges and universities including many CCCU institutions, and is regularly selected for inclusion in the Best Lawyers in America listing. Lowell also served for ten years in the administration of Taylor University in the positions of Residence Hall Director, Director of Student Programs, Dean of Students, Vice President for Student Development and now serves as a member of the Board of Trustees. Lowell earned an MA in Student Personnel Administration in Higher Education from Ball State University, and a JD from Indiana University. Lowell is a regular speaker and author on higher education topics.

Timothy Herrmann is a Professor and Graduate Director of the MA in Higher Education and Student Development program at Taylor University. Tim has also served in a variety of other roles including Dean of Assessment, Associate Professor of Psychology, and Associate Dean of Students. In each of these roles a primary goal has been to promote healthy collaboration between the various administrative divisions of the university. A past-president of the Association for Christians in Student Development and co-founder/co-editor of *Growth: The Journal of the Association for Christian in Student Development*, Tim earned a BA in history from Taylor University, an MA in counseling from Ohio State University, and a PhD in higher education administration from Indiana State University. He is co-author of the recently published *Parents Guide to the Christian College: Supporting your Child's Heart, Soul, and Mind during the College Years* (ACU Press, 2011).

Shirley A. Mullen currently serves as President of Houghton College. Born and raised in eastern Canada, Shirley graduated *summa cum laude* from Houghton College in 1976 and went on to earn a MA in history from the University of Toronto. In 1985, she completed a PhD in history from the University of Minnesota, and in 2000 a second doctorate in philosophy from the University of Wales. Shirley spent the first twenty-three years of her academic career teaching European history at Westmont College in Santa Barbara, California. Her special areas of interest are the Enlightenment tradition, the Victorian period in England, and David Hume. After serving as Provost at Westmont for four years, in June of 2006, Shirley accepted an invitation to return to her alma mater as its fifth president. Shirley serves as a Fuller Theological Seminary Trustee, on the National Association of Evangelicals Board, and on the Allegany County United Way Board.

Albert J. Meyer, a long-time faculty member who served for many years as CEO of the Mennonite Board of Education and as a coordinator with the Committee on Liberal Arts Education of the North Central Association of Colleges and Secondary Schools. He has also been a Visiting Fellow at the Center for the Study of American

Religion, Princeton University. His publications include *Realizing Our Intentions: A Guide for Churches and Colleges with Distinctive Missions* (ACU Press, 2009) on the subject of retaining a commitment to educational missions. He now lives in Goshen, Indiana.

Lois J. Voigt has served for more than twenty years as a chief financial officer in three different higher educational institutions, most recently at Messiah College. She also worked in accounting and management positions in two Fortune 500 companies, serves on several not-for-profit boards, and has presented on a variety of higher educational topics at regional and national conferences. Lois earned a BA from the University of Sioux Falls, an MBA from the University of Colorado, and a PhD in higher educational administration from Loyola University of Chicago.